Secrets to Writing a Fantasy

The Supernatural Structure

Write Novels That Sell: Volume 4

by K. Stanley and L. Cooke

While every precaution has been taken in the preparation of this book, the publisher assumes no responsibility for errors or omissions, or for damages resulting from the use of the information contained herein.

SECRETS TO WRITING A FANTASY

First edition. April 20, 2025.

Copyright © 2025 K. Stanley and L. Cooke.

ISBN: 978-1738022137

Written by K. Stanley and L. Cooke.

Table of Contents

Secrets to Writing a Fantasy (Write Novels That Sell, #4) 1

PART ONE 7

Chapter One: Introduction 9

Chapter Two: Speculative Fiction and Fantasy 17

Chapter Three: Meet the Process 27

Chapter Four: The External Plot 35

Chapter Five: The Supernatural Plot 47

Chapter Six: Create your External Plot Skeleton Synopsis 53

Chapter Seven: Create Your Supernatural Skeleton Synopsis 70

Chapter Eight: Combined Skeleton Blurb 87

Chapter Nine: Weaving a Fantasy Story 93

PART TWO 127

Chapter Ten: Fantasy Genre-Specific Patterns 129

Chapter Eleven: Opening Image & Opening Chapter 133

Chapter Twelve: Lead-Up to the External Inciting Incident 144

Chapter Thirteen: External Inciting Incident 150

Chapter Fourteen: Reaction to the External Inciting Incident 158

Chapter Fifteen: Lead-Up to the Supernatural Inciting Incident. 163

Chapter Sixteen: Supernatural Inciting Incident 168

Chapter Seventeen: Reaction to the Supernatural Inciting Incident 175

Chapter Eighteen: Resistance to the Story Goal 180

Chapter Nineteen: Lead-Up to the External Plot Point 1 185

Chapter Twenty: External Plot Point 1 Adventure Accepted 191

Chapter Twenty-One: Reaction to the External Plot Point 1 197

Chapter Twenty-Two: Lead-up to the Supernatural Plot Point 1 203

Chapter Twenty-Three: Supernatural Plot Point 1 207

Chapter Twenty-Four: Reaction to the Supernatural Plot Point 1 213

Chapter Twenty-Five: Goal Attempts 218

Chapter Twenty-Six: Lead-Up to the External Middle Plot Point 229

Chapter Twenty-Seven: External Middle Plot Point 233

Chapter Twenty-Eight: Reaction to the External Middle Plot Point 238

Chapter Twenty-Nine: Lead-Up to the Supernatural Middle Plot Point 243

Chapter Thirty: Supernatural Middle Plot Point 248

Chapter Thirty-One: Reaction to the Supernatural Middle Plot Point 254

Chapter Thirty-Two: External Pressures 258

Chapter Thirty-Three: Lead-Up to the External Plot Point 2 267

Chapter Thirty-Four: External Plot Point 2 272

Chapter Thirty-Five: Reaction to the External Plot Point 2 279

Chapter Thirty-Six: Lead-Up to the Supernatural Plot Point 2 ... 283

Chapter Thirty-Seven: Supernatural Plot Point 2 287

Chapter Thirty-Eight: Reaction to the Supernatural Plot Point 2 291

Chapter Thirty-Nine: Protagonist Understands the Story Goal .. 295

Chapter Forty: Lead-Up to the External Climax 301

Chapter Forty-One: External Climax 305

Chapter Forty-Two: Reaction to the External Climax 310

Chapter Forty-Three: Lead-Up to the Supernatural Climax 313

Chapter Forty-Four: The Supernatural Climax 316

Chapter Forty-Five: Reaction to the Supernatural Climax 320

Chapter Forty-Six: Resolution 324

Chapter Forty-Seven: Closing Image 328

PART THREE 332

Chapter Forty-Eight: The Story Arc Supporting Scenes 334

Chapter Forty-Nine: Are You Writing a Series or a Single Novel? 350

Appendix: Fantasy Decisions 354

Appendix: Fantasy Checklist 361

Acknowledgments 370

About the Authors..371

By K. Stanley and L. Cooke

Secrets to Editing Success: The Creative Story Editing Method

(Book 1: Write Novels That Sell)

Published February 2023

Secrets to Outlining a Novel: The Creative Outlining Method

(Book 2: Write Novels That Sell)

Published September 2023

Secrets to Writing a Series: The Creative Series Writing Method

(Book 3: Write Novels That Sell)

Published July 2024

Secrets to Writing a Fantasy: The Supernatural Structure

(Book 4: Write Novels That Sell)

Published January 2025

By K. Stanley

Descent

Blaze

Avalanche

The Author's Guide to Selling Books to Non-Bookstore

Praise for the Write Novels That Sell Series

Praise for *Secrets to Writing a Fantasy: The Supernatural Structure*

A Clear & Practical Guide for Fantasy Authors: This book offers a clear and straightforward approach to writing a fantasy novel, breaking down (what can sometimes be) complex storytelling elements into smaller, more manageable steps. K. Stanley and L. Cooke explain not only what makes fantasy novels work but also why each element matters to the bigger story—and they support their methodology with relevant examples from bestselling fantasy novels, too. Like their previous writing guides, this book combines practical instruction with clear explanations, making it an essential resource for both aspiring and experienced fantasy writers. Highly recommend!

—**Savannah Gilbo, Developmental Editor and Book Coach.**

K. Stanley and L. Cooke have written the definitive guide to structuring a fantasy novel!

—**USA Today Bestselling Author Kit Morgan**

Praise for Secretsto Writing a Series: The Creative Series Writing Method

"The clear, step-by-step approach of Secrets to Writing a Series will take you from idea to epic, regardless of series length."

—**Carol Fisher Saller, Editor and Author of Maddie's Ghost**

Praise for *Secrets to Editing Success: The Creative Story Editing Method*

"One of the most frequent questions a novelist asks is, 'Does my draft contain a story?' Stanley and Cooke have written a practical guide that shows you how to answer that question. Secrets to Editing Success gives you actionable advice and a process to edit and revise your novel so that you can take your novel draft and turn it into a publishable book."

—**Grant Faulkner, executive director of National Novel Writing Month**

"Secrets to Editing Success is every editor's dream. Whether you're a new author reviewing your first book or a professional editor, this is without doubt the most comprehensive and detailed guide to editing I've ever had the pleasure of reading. This book will hold your hand, explain, clarify, and give you step-by-step instructions for editing your novel. Paired best when using the incomparable developmental editing software Fictionary, this guide will change your editing life. Read it. Immediately."

—**Sacha Black, Rebel Author Podcast**

Praise *for Secrets to Outlining a Novel: The Creative Outlining Method*

"A fresh, actionable, step-by-clear-step approach to creating a story outline that produces amazing results! Can't sing enough praises for Secrets to Outlining a Novel. Don't write your next novel without these insights, hints, and tips."

—**Mary Buckham, USA Today bestselling author of Break into Fiction: 11 Steps to Building a Powerful Story**

"Writing a book is a huge (and scary) task. In Secrets to Outlining a Novel, Kristina, and Lucy have demystified the process, breaking it down into approachable, bite-size pieces that help you understand outlining at both a macro and micro level."

—**Hayley Milliman, Head of Education, ProWritingAid**

Dedications

This book is dedicated to my husband Mathew. Without him, there is nothing.

—K. Stanley

To Edward and William,

Both of you are pure magic.

—L. Cooke

PART ONE
Fantasy Story Foundations

Chapter One: Introduction

"Let's write a book about the structure of commercially successful fantasy novels," Kristina said.

"It'll be magic," Lucy said. "After all, we both love dragons, fairies, spells, witches, wizards, potions, alchemy, mythical worlds, and epic storytelling."

We knew when the supernatural is part of a book, that book becomes a fantasy. Using this, we had a single burning question: "How do you structure a novel that includes the supernatural?"

To answer this question, our research took us to our favorite place: books. We did what we love doing and studied the deep structure of commercially successful fantasy novels.

We built on our knowledge of story structure and reverse-outlined commercially successful books to reveal the fantasy story structure, and we want to share our insights with you. By the end of this book, if you do the fun tasks, you'll have created the foundation for a structurally sound fantasy novel. So get ready to be creative.

Combining your imagination with our process will get your readers loving your fantasy book and begging you to write more. Your writing and our process is a mix that will make your stories magic. Reading this book does not guarantee a novel will be commercially successful, but it will show you how commercially successful novels are structured. And that is a wealth of information.

Every time you see an unlock symbol, we'll share a secret we uncovered. Let's get to the first secret.

Commercially successful fantasy novels contain genre-specific patterns.

Not only will we show you what the patterns are, we'll show you how to weave them together. We will go into depth about these scenes in Chapter Three: Meet the Process and Chapter 10: Fantasy Genre-Specific Patterns. At the moment, hold with the idea that a reader subconsciously expects scenes in a story, and if these scenes are not there, the reader will feel something is missing.

Each step of the way, we're here to help you create a unique story that only you can write. By the end of this book, you'll have a creation method, and with that, you can write as many fantasy books as your imagination allows.

This doesn't guarantee that you'll write a commercially successful novel too. Our goal is to give you enough knowledge and show you examples to clarify that knowledge so you can write a commercially successful novel.

How to Use This Book

We love a logical process, especially for writing a novel. Fantasy stories are wonderfully complex affairs. Readers travel through pages of supernatural encounters, epic journeys, and jaw-clenching subplots with characters they connect with, care about, and hope will harness the supernatural.

SECRETS TO WRITING A FANTASY

In a fantasy novel, readers want to experience the protagonist harnessing the supernatural.

We've just given you the first of many genre-specific patterns. Read on to find out where those patterns occur in a novel.

Our process will not limit your creativity. This method is filled with activities that will ignite ideas and speed up your writing.

This book is for fantasy writers who have an idea, are ready to outline, are writing, or already editing their novel. This book is for you, no matter the stage of writing you are at.

We believe the whole writing journey should be both enjoyable and confidence-building. After all, writing takes bravery. And bravery is so much easier if you feel you've done your best. With our process, you'll know that with absolute certainty.

For this book, we narrowed down the novels we studied and chose those that best represent different types of fantasy novels.

To ensure we found that deep structure, we chose novels with different levels of magic or mythical creatures, protagonist strategies, and POV strategies. This gave us a broad range that represents the most common types of story strategies. We checked the theory against many other commercially successful fantasy novels and were thrilled with how many contain the same structure.

Commercially successful fantasy novels all include a supernatural plot.

This seems obvious, but that is part of the process. Making straightforward choices at the start will lead you to decisions that will end up in a unique book that only you can write, with a structure that is what a reader is expecting.

To ensure we found that deep structure, we chose novels with different levels of magic or mythical creatures, protagonist strategies, and POV strategies. This gave us a broad range that represents the most common types of story strategies. This book contains an in-depth look at six novels. We checked the theory against many other commercially successful fantasy novels and were thrilled with how many contain the same structure.

From these examples, you'll learn how commercially successful stories are structured and how to create that structure.

Fantasy Novel Examples and Analysis

Examples are a great way to learn, so we'll explore six commercially successful fantasy novels. The books have subgenres in romance, dark fantasy, urban fantasy, epic fantasy, and military fantasy.

When we discuss novels containing the supernatural, we're referring to fantasy worlds where magic contains a system of rules and powers and often exists alongside mythical creatures like dragons, vampires, and elves. These novels can also contain mythical creatures but no magic.

We'll take you through the process described in this book and show how it applies to each of the novels.

Please note we are going to study each of these novels in depth and there will be spoilers. We will reveal the endings. These are all novels to read if you're interested in story structure and how it works.

The books are:

Fourth Wing **by Rebecca Yarros**

Fourth Wing takes place in the country of Navarre. In this world, every young person enters one of four quadrants in a college: Scribes, Riders (dragon riders), Healers, or Infantry. In the Riders Quadrant, humans bond with dragons. Once the bonding is in place, the dragon rider receives a signet, a new power a rider gains from their dragon. Violet is the protagonist. She enters the Riders Quadrant with the goal of surviving the first year. These elite riders protect Navarre's borders from other mythical creatures.

The novel is a fantasy novel because it contains magic, dragons, and other mythical creatures.

Twilight **by Stephenie Meyer**

Twilight is set in a small town called Forks in northwest Washington State, USA. The protagonist, Bella, moves to Forks and soon discovers supernatural forces at play. The mythical creatures are vampires who hide from the sun. The rainy northwest facilitates this. Once Bella falls in love with a vampire, her goal is to find a way to live with vampires and not die.

The novel is a fantasy novel because there are vampires and werewolves.

The Unbroken **by C. L. Clark**

This story takes place in the Balladaire Empire. Touraine, the protagonist, was stolen as a child and trained to be infantry for the Balladaire Empire. She returns to her home as a soldier expected to protect the empire against her home. The supernatural comes into this story from the Shālan magic, and both the protagonist and her main love interest spend the first book trying to discover the healing magic.

The novel is a fantasy novel because there is magic in the story

A Court of Thorns and Roses by Sarah J. Maas

The magic realm of Prythian is divided into seven courts: the Spring, Summer, Autumn, Winter, Day, Night, and Dawn courts. Mortals live in the south and west of Prythian. The protagonist, Feyre, kills a fairy and as penance must live forever in Prythian. Her goal is to escape and return home.

The novel is a fantasy novel because it contains magic as well as mythical creatures.

Legendborn by Tracy Deonn

This urban fantasy is set at the University of North Carolina, Chapel Hill campus. In the opening scenes, the protagonist is notified that her mother is dead. Bree enters a college underworld of magic and is determined to find out who killed her mother.

The novel is a fantasy novel because magic and mythical creatures are in the story. There are Shadowborn creatures that the Legendborn must guard against.

A Game of Thrones by George R. R. Martin

The realm of the seven kingdoms is set in the continent of Westeros. The Westeros history is vast. This is a complex story where the kingdoms must come together to fight against the White Walkers. The mythical creatures have long been in hiding and are now coming to annihilate the humans. This is an epic battle of humans against mythical creatures.

The novel is a fantasy novel because there are magic and mythical creatures in the story.

Chapter Two: Speculative Fiction and Fantasy

There are many types of stories, and genres give the reader a hint of what type of story they are about to read.

Each reader brings their own experience to the story and may read the book as one genre when the author intended it as another. And that's ok. Genre descriptions are flexible and open to interpretation. Think of genre as a spectrum; some stories are slap bang in the center of a genre, others are to one side or the other. But they all have something that unites them.

Our goal as authors is to write the story we want to tell and use genre guidelines to help us write a story that readers want to read.

Speculative fiction is a story that takes place in an unknown world. Something exists in the fictional world that does not exist in the world we (humans) live in. This includes magic, mythical creatures, or technology.

Fantasy, horror, and science fiction fall into the speculative fiction category. The story within the pages transports the reader to a world filled with wonder, excitement, and thrills. Yet, a fantasy novel differs from a horror novel, which differs from a science fiction novel.

In fantasy or horror novels, the reader assumes that the natural laws of Earth don't apply.

In science fiction, when technology is used that doesn't exist in our world, the reader will assume the natural laws of Earth apply.

Fantasy should take the reader on an adventure. It's often about a world where something is terribly wrong. That's where the story begins. Fantasy can contain a rational magic system or an irrational one. A rational magic system means we can understand it. Irrational means we can't.

Horror should frighten the reader with the unknown. The story is often about a monster that doesn't exist in the world today. The goal of the protagonist is to survive. Horror usually contains an irrational magic system.

Science fiction should intrigue the reader by using technology. It looks at what could be in our world but isn't. New technology plays a large part in this story. If characters use technology that doesn't exist on Earth today, the story is science fiction. In pure science fiction, only existing life on Earth can be found in the book.

One story can contain all three genres, and the genres blur into one another. This book shows how to write a fantasy novel. We won't cover science fiction, horror, or a combination of genres.

Let's start by looking at our definition of the supernatural.

The Supernatural: Our Definition

These are our definitions, and we created them, so we all have the same understanding of the concepts. If you don't agree with them, that's ok. It's more important that you know how we're thinking about the terms.

What Is Supernatural in a Fantasy Novel?

SECRETS TO WRITING A FANTASY

In this book, when we refer to the supernatural, we mean magic, mythical creatures, or both. Within magic, we include powers such as telekinesis, levitation, precognition and extrasensory perception.

A novel must include magic, mythical creatures, or both; otherwise, it's not a fantasy.

Readers are reading for this aspect. When you write your fantasy, monitoring the supernatural plot is key to unlocking your story's potential.

A compelling supernatural system in a fantasy novel requires several key ingredients. Readers want to see protagonists grapple with the fundamental principles and control of magic or mythical creatures.

The supernatural is a journey of discovery, both for the reader and the protagonist. This journey, however, thrives on structure. Defined rules for the supernatural create a sense of wonder.

Magic

This is not a book on how to create magic or mythical creatures. It's about the structure of a fantasy novel that is often found in bestsellers.

That said, as the author, you hold the power to define the very essence of magic in your world. Here are some key decisions to consider:

- The source of the magic.
- Magic limitations.

- Magical costs. Magic shouldn't be priceless.

Mythical Creatures

Not every fantasy world relies solely on magic systems to create their supernatural element. Some authors weave their wonder through mythical creatures. From dragons and unicorns to fairies and werewolves, these fantastical beings make the novel part of the fantasy genre.

Structurally, mythical creatures need to be introduced to the reader in the same way any character is introduced.

Here are some key questions to answer:

- Does the protagonist know about the mythical creatures?

- Do the mythical creatures help or hinder the protagonist in their attempt to reach the external or supernatural story goal?

- What limitations do the mythical creatures have?

Fantasy Novel Structure Explained

What is Story Structure?

Story structure is the order in which you place the scenes in your novel. But that's not all. Strong story structure is about placing the right scenes in the right place, where each scene performs the right duties.

Story structure is about form and not about formula, and it starts with the five story arc scenes. The five story arc scenes form the foundation of your plot. These are the inciting incident, plot point 1, the middle plot point, plot point 2, and the climax. If one of the five story arc scenes is missing, there is no story yet.

We have the biggest secret of all when writing a fantasy.

Fantasy novels all include an external and a supernatural story.

All stories have an external plot. The protagonist has an external story goal with external story stakes if they don't achieve that goal. In a fantasy, there is another plot line. The same protagonist must also have a supernatural story goal with supernatural story stakes.

This means there are five story arc scenes for the external plot plus five story arc scenes for the supernatural plot. By the time you've worked through this book, you'll create all the scenes your story needs.

To do this, you'll create the main events for both the external and supernatural story arc scenes. By weaving the external and supernatural scenes, you'll create a fantasy novel structured in a way that readers will remember your story.

Before we cover the genre-specific patterns, let's define a scene.

A Scene

A scene is a unit of story where characters engage in action and dialogue. In each scene, you'll find a purpose and a POV character. The POV character has a goal for the scene. A powerful scene begins with an entry hook that draws the reader into the scene. Each scene ends with the reader knowing if the POV character achieved the POV goal or not.

Here is the rundown of how a scene should be structured.

At the start:

- An entry hook draws the reader into the scene.

- The POV goal shows the reader what the character will try to achieve in the scene.

In the middle of the scene:

- The action changes direction and possibly includes an obstacle for the protagonist to overcome.

At the end of the scene:

- The reader discovers whether the POV character achieved their scene goal.

- An exit hook propels the reader into the next scene.

The Purpose of Each Scene

A scene's purpose is the reason the scene exists in the story. We'll go one level deeper and show you the purpose of scenes specific to a fantasy novel.

Every scene in a fantasy novel must have a purpose related to the external or supernatural story goal.

External and Supernatural Plots

Let's take a moment to review definitions because a common understanding is key to success.

The External Plot

The external plot contains scenes where the protagonist:

- Is given a challenge.
- Accepts the adventure caused by the challenge.
- Experiences a false victory or defeat.
- Faces dark forces.
- Addresses the challenge for the final time.

These five scenes show the function of the external inciting incident, plot point 1, middle plot point, plot point 2, and climax.

The Supernatural Plot

The supernatural plot contains scenes where the protagonist:

- Gets an inkling that the supernatural elements exist or an inkling they can influence the supernatural.

- Believes in or uses the supernatural to try to attain the story goal.

- Proactively uses the supernatural.

- Discovers the supernatural has limitations.

- Uses the supernatural in their final attempt to achieve the supernatural story goal.

These five scenes show the function of the supernatural inciting incident, plot point 1, middle plot point, plot point 2, and climax.

Take a moment to digest what this means. You'll be writing a story that contains two story arcs. Isn't this empowering?

Example Novels: External and Supernatural Plots

The easiest way to summarize a plot is to create a skeleton blurb. This is one sentence that shows who the protagonist is, what their goal is, and what's at stake if they cannot achieve the goal.

A fantasy novel needs an external and supernatural skeleton blurb.

Let's look at our six novels. These are the skeleton blurbs we wrote for each book.

Fourth Wing by Rebecca Yarros

External Plot: Violet must use her intelligence to fight other students in the Riders Quadrant; otherwise, she won't survive her first year as a cadet.

Supernatural Plot: Violet must learn to control her signet; otherwise, she can't protect Navarre's borders from evil mythical creatures and all inside the borders will die.

Twilight by Stephenie Meyer

External Plot: Bella must learn to live with her father in a new town; otherwise, her mother will not have a new life.

Supernatural Plot: Bella must learn to live among vampires; otherwise, she will not find her "Happy Ever After" life with Edward.

The Unbroken by C. L. Clark

External Plot: Touraine must choose the winning side in the battle between the empire, her homeland, and the Shālan; otherwise, she will die.

Supernatural Plot: Touraine must learn Shālan magic; otherwise, her people will die.

A Court of Thorns and Roses by Sarah J. Maas

External Plot: Feyre must find a way to leave Prythian; otherwise, she will never see her family again.

Supernatural Plot: Feyre must break an ancient curse; otherwise, she will doom her lover's world, and she will die.

Legendborn by Tracy Deonn

External Plot: Bree must search for the truth about her mother's death; otherwise, she won't understand her heritage and how to live among the supernatural.

Supernatural Plot: Bree must combine root magic with Legendborn magic; otherwise, the ancient ones will destroy the world.

A Game of Thrones by George R. R. Martin

External Plot: The humans must choose who will sit on the throne; otherwise; the kingdoms will fall apart.

Supernatural Plot: The humans must leverage the supernatural; otherwise, they can't beat the White Walkers, and they all die.

Skeleton Blurb Patterns

Five of the novels have stakes that are personal to the protagonist in the external plot and have larger stakes related to the world in the supernatural plot.

Chapter Three: Meet the Process

We've created a process specific to the fantasy genre that will help you at every stage of story creation. Our process is not meant to dictate the order you work.

Why Have a Process?

A process to write a story is critical to keep you on track with the story, with your time, and with your creativity.

What a Process Is Not

A process is not a formula. The process we are showing you is a form that you can use to create the story you want to write. If there are aspects to the process that don't resonate, then remember, you are the artist. Understand you have the final word for what goes into your story.

We'll show you the why and the how, and you choose what part of the process resonates. We must say, we have cut the process to what we know as the necessities for a strong structure.

If you find a part of the process tough, ask if it is because you don't have the answer yet. If that is the case, then that's ok. You can either hold the answer you have right now loosely and give yourself permission to change your mind later on, or you can move on to the next stage, coming back when inspiration arrives.

Understanding the Why

Understanding that a fantasy novel needs both an external and a supernatural plot gives you a solid foundation and will help you unlock your story.

Fantasy is a perfect balance of an external plot, which is universal to any narrative, and a supernatural plot. These two plot lines are woven together.

A story without an external plot is not a story. A story without a supernatural plot is not a fantasy.

If your creative muse is all about the external plot, follow that creative call. Once that's outlined, create the supernatural plot. For a different story, it could be the magic and mythical creatures that inspire you, and that plot line appears before you even sit down to write it. Please start with that one.

Whether you're writing about magic or mythical creatures, the supernatural, they need structure. The reader needs enough information to believe and understand the supernatural aspect of the story.

This book is going to take you through fun tasks, so work along with us, and you'll create a strong foundation for your fantasy novel.

You'll create:

- An external plot skeleton blurb
- A supernatural plot skeleton blurb
- The external plot story arc scenes

SECRETS TO WRITING A FANTASY

- The supernatural plot story arc scenes
- A combined skeleton blurb

And when you've done all that, you'll weave the story arc scenes. After the story arc scenes are woven, it's time to consider the genre-specific patterns.

Decision: How much of the supernatural will you explain?

As the writer, you know everything about the supernatural world in your story. The reader only knows what you show them, and that means their experience differs from yours, but you can still control that experience. You decide what level of detail is important to your story.

Decision: Who controls the supernatural?

Which character can control or influence the supernatural elements in the story? The stronger the supernatural structure, the more a character can control it. The more difficult the supernatural structure is to understand, the more the characters have to rely on their convictions, strengths, or intuition.

In *Fourth Wing*, each cadet controls unique magic through their dragon.

In *The Unbroken*, the healers control the healing magic.

In *Twilight*, Bella is protected from the vampires because of her relationship with Edward.

In *A Game of Thorns and Roses*, the fairies have magic and humans don't.

In *Legendborn*, descendants of Arthur or of the women with root magic control the magic.

In *Game of Thrones*, different characters control different supernatural elements.

Each novel is set up differently, and yours will be too. Once you make decisions, be careful to stay consistent.

Decision: How will you show the supernatural in a series?

This is not a book about how to write a series, but since many fantasy novels are part of a series, we thought we should share a tip. In every new book in a series, the protagonist needs a new hurdle to overcome relating to the supernatural. If you show everything about the supernatural in book one of your series, there is nothing new to show in future books.

In book one, the protagonist might want to live with the supernatural, then in book two the protagonist might have to try to live without the supernatural. This is the Twilight series structure.

It might be that in book one, characters meet the supernatural and understand how to wield it in a particular way. Then in book two, the rules change, and these new complications mean that the protagonist must learn all over again. This is the structure of the *Fourth Wing* and *Iron Flame* books from The Empyrean series.

Genre-Specific Patterns

We've given you a high-level process. Now we'll focus on what is needed to finish the rest of the novel. Before we move forward, let's look at the genre-specific patterns. You'll work on scenes that contain these patterns after you weave the external and supernatural story arc scenes.

The order of the scenes is dictated by their purpose. You decide where you want the scenes to be. You may find that some scenes listed below can be combined into one scene, or that they need multiple scenes to serve the story. For now, we're looking for the main event that happens in these scenes. Later in this book, you'll see how these scenes are woven into the six novels we've chosen.

The following shows the scenes required for both the external and supernatural plots. Some of these will be the same scenes for both storylines. For example, there can be only one opening image and one closing image.

Every novel has only one opening image and one closing image.

Opening Image

Lead-Up to the External Inciting Incident

EXTERNAL INCITING INCIDENT: The Challenge

Reaction to the External Inciting Incident

Resistance to the External Story Goal

Lead-Up to the Supernatural Inciting Incident

SUPERNATURAL INCITING INCIDENT: Inkling the Supernatural Exists

Reaction to the Supernatural Inciting Incident

Resistance to the Supernatural Story Goal

Lead-Up to External Plot Point 1

EXTERNAL PLOT POINT 1: Adventure Accepted

Reaction to External Plot Point 1

Lead-Up to Supernatural Plot Point 1

SUPERNATURAL PLOT POINT 1: Believes In or Uses the Supernatural

Reaction to Supernatural Plot Point 1

Goal Attempt 1

Goal Attempt 2

Goal Attempt 3

Lead-Up to the External Middle Plot Point

EXTERNAL MIDDLE PLOT POINT: False Victory or Defeat

Reaction to the External Middle Plot Point

Lead-Up to the Supernatural Middle Plot Point

SUPERNATURAL MIDDLE PLOT POINT: Proactively Uses the Supernatural

Reaction to the Supernatural Middle Plot Point

External Pressures 1

External Pressures 2

External Pressures 3

Lead-Up to External Plot Point 2

EXTERNAL PLOT POINT 2: Dark Forces

Reaction to External Plot Point 2

Lead-Up to the Supernatural Plot Point 2

SUPERNATURAL PLOT POINT 2: Supernatural Limitation

Reaction to the Supernatural Plot Point 2

Protagonist Understands the Story Goal

Lead-Up to the External Climax

EXTERNAL CLIMAX: Achieves External Goal or Not

Reaction to the External Climax

Lead-Up to the Supernatural Climax

SUPERNATURAL CLIMAX: Uses the Supernatural to Achieve Goal

Reaction to the Supernatural Climax

Resolution

Closing Image

The Fantasy Vault

Part of the process is to keep a record of your decisions. These decisions should be kept in a safe place for you to come back to after you've outlined, written, edited, or even published your novel.

We recommend that you create your fantasy vault along with us. This will be your guide should you want to revisit your story with a sequel, a prequel, or another book based in this world or with these characters.

You'll start with decisions you make while outlining, then add new decisions while you're writing, and add more decisions while you're editing. Your fantasy vault is an ever-evolving space. When your book is published, you'll have a record of every decision you've made for your story.

Chapter Four: The External Plot

Every story must have an external plot. The reader must understand that the protagonist is striving for something external and learn if the protagonist is successful or not at the end of the story. Create a strong external story goal, and the reader will think, *Yep, I want to find out if the protagonist is successful or not.*

An external plot shows the protagonist's movement through the story. The stakes are the reason they put themselves in tension-filled situations and why they risk everything to achieve their story goal. It's not enough to hook a reader. If the protagonist fails to achieve the external goal, there must be consequences.

In *Fourth Wing*, the stakes are clear in the first pages. Violet will die if she doesn't achieve the external story goal.

Create an External Plot Skeleton Blurb

Creating a skeleton blurb is the first step. Please don't skip it. You can update the skeleton blurb as your story changes, but for now, it's your starting point.

Skeleton Blurb Definition

Skeleton blurbs are a tool for you, the writer. A skeleton blurb is the shortest version of a story blurb that answers:

1. Who is the protagonist?
2. What is their goal?

3. What is at stake?

The Protagonist:

This is more complicated than it first seems. The next section shows you how to determine who the protagonist is and what type of protagonist they are.

The Story Goal:

This is what the protagonist wants to achieve in the story. The goal must be clear enough that the reader can answer whether the protagonist reached that goal in the climax scene.

The Stakes:

This is what will be lost if the protagonist does not achieve the story goal. In a fantasy novel, the stakes are usually life and death.

The Purpose of a Skeleton Blurb

This is a tool to use as you outline, write, and edit your novel. Its purpose is:

1. To keep you focused as you outline, write, and edit.
2. To know if every scene belongs in your novel.

Fantasy Skeleton Blurbs

You'll write more than one skeleton blurb. Here's the list:

1. External plot skeleton blurb.
2. Supernatural plot skeleton blurb.
3. Subplot skeleton blurbs (there can be more than one).

That means you'll need at least two skeleton blurbs for your fantasy novel and maybe more, depending on how many subplots are in the story.

For example, the *Fourth Wing* skeleton blurbs we wrote are:

External Plot: Violet Sorrengail must use her intelligence to fight other students in the Riders Quadrant; otherwise, she won't survive her first year as a cadet.

Supernatural Plot: Violet must learn to control her signet; otherwise, she can't protect Navarre's borders from evil mythical creatures and all inside the borders will die.

Romance Subplot: Violet must learn to trust Xaden; otherwise, they will never find their "Happy Ever After" moment.

Each of these skeleton blurbs are for plot lines that will require story arc scenes.

The Protagonist

When you're outlining, your point of view strategy helps determine who the protagonist is. When you're editing, reviewing the number of scenes each character has as the point of view character will show if you've got the balance correct.

There are three types of protagonists.

Single Protagonist: One character has a story goal, and there are story stakes related to that goal.

Combined Protagonist: Two characters have the same story goal with the same stakes.

Group Protagonist: Multiple characters have the same story goal, but the stakes are different for each of them.

How to Find the Protagonist

When you're outlining, it will help if you know who your protagonist is before you begin. That's the only way you can write a skeleton blurb.

When you're editing a draft, you'll want to check that the structure of your story is strong based on the type of protagonist you chose.

We use a combination of data points to determine who the protagonist is.

- The number of scenes in a novel shows us the scope of the story.

- The number of scenes written from each character's point of view shows us who the potential protagonists are.

- The point of view character for the opening can also help us decide, but it isn't a clear indicator.

Let's review our example novels and find the protagonist.

Building External Plot Skeleton Blurbs

Fourth Wing by Rebecca Yarros

Fourth Wing is a fantasy novel with a strong romance between two characters. The love interests are Violet Sorrengail and Xaden Rhiorson.

Violet's external skeleton blurb is:

Violet Sorrengail must use her intelligence to survive the Riders Quadrant; otherwise, she will not survive her first year as a cadet.

Xaden's external skeleton blurb is:

Xaden Rhiorson must keep Violet alive; otherwise; her mother will execute all of his friends.

The goal is similar, but the stakes are different.

At a glance, either of these could be the protagonist. There are seventy-three scenes in this novel. Seventy-one of these scenes are written from Violet's point of view, and two are written from Xaden's. That's a sound argument that Violet is the protagonist.

The opening image is written from Violet's point of view. This is another clue that Violet is the protagonist.

All the above shows Violet is the single protagonist in *Fourth Wing*.

Twilight by Stephenie Meyer

In *Twilight* the love interests are Bella Swan and Edward Cullen. The fantasy and romance plots cannot be removed from the story. If the romance is removed, the novel fits in the horror genre. If the vampire aspect is removed, the novel fits in the young adult romance genre.

Bella's external skeleton blurb is:

Bella must learn to live with her father in a new town; otherwise, her mother will not have a new life.

Edward's external skeleton blurb is:

Edward must hide that is he a vampire; otherwise, he can't coexist with humans.

Both the goals and the stakes are different. One of the characters must be the protagonist.

There are thirty scenes and all, including the opening image, are written from Bella's point of view.

This means Bella is the single protagonist.

The Unbroken by C. L. Clark

The Unbroken is a military fantasy. The subplot is a romance between Touraine and Luca.

Touraine's external skeleton blurb is:

Touraine must choose the winning side in the battle between the empire, her homeland, and the Shālan; otherwise, she will die.

Luca's skeleton blurb is:

Luca must stop the rebellion; otherwise, she won't become queen.

Because Touraine and Luca have different goals and stakes for the story, only one is the protagonist.

The opening image is written from Touraine's point of view. The reader meets her before they meet Luca. This is a hint that Touraine is the protagonist.

There are one hundred and seven scenes. Sixty-four of the scenes are written from Touraine's point of view, and forty-three are written from Luca's point of view. This means sixty percent of the scenes are written from Touraine's point of view.

When we put this together, we are shown that Touraine is the single protagonist.

A Court of Thorns and Roses by Sarah J. Maas

A Court of Thorns and Roses is an epic/high fantasy with a romance subplot. The love interests are Feyre and Tamlin.

Feyre's external skeleton blurb is:

Feyre must find a way to leave Prythian; otherwise, she will never see her family again.

Tamlin's skeleton blurb is:

Tamlin must make a human love him; otherwise, his world is doomed.

Feyre and Tamlin have different goals and stakes, so only one is the protagonist.

All the scenes are written from Feyre's point of view, including the opening image.

This shows us Feyre is the single protagonist.

Legendborn by Tracy Deonn

Legendborn is a contemporary fantasy with a romance subplot. The love interests are Bree and Nick.

Bree's external skeleton blurb is:

Bree must search for the truth about her mother's death; otherwise, she won't understand her heritage and how to live among the supernatural.

Nick's external skeleton blurb is:

Nick must reclaim his title as king; otherwise, humans will cease to exist.

Bree and Nick have different goals and stakes, meaning one of them is the protagonist.

Bree is the point of view character for every scene, therefore she is the protagonist.

A Game of Thrones by George R. R. Martin

A Game of Thrones is a dark fantasy. There are nine POV characters in the first book.

These are Eddard Stark, Catelyn Stark, Daenerys Targaryen, Tyrion Lannister, Jon Snow, Bran Stark, Sansa Stark, Arya Stark, and Will. Each of these characters has a skeleton blurb.

Seven of the POV characters have an external skeleton blurb. Two have a supernatural skeleton blurb.

External Skeleton Blurbs

Eddard Stark must protect the existing King; otherwise, the wrong king will sit on the throne.

Catelyn Stark must find out who is behind Bran's murder attempt; otherwise, the Lannisters will sit on the throne.

Tyrion Lannister must use his intelligence to win political games; otherwise, the wrong leader will sit on the throne.

SECRETS TO WRITING A FANTASY

Jon Snow must go to the Night's Watch; otherwise, he can't protect the North and many will die.

Sansa Stark must learn to play political games; otherwise, she won't sit on the throne with Joffrey.

Arya Stark must learn to become a warrior; otherwise, the wrong king will sit on the throne.

Will must hide; otherwise, he will die.

Supernatural Skeleton Blurbs

Daenerys must become the mother of dragons; otherwise, she won't become the Dothraki leader and she will die.

Bran Stark must learn to use his seeing ability; otherwise; he will die.

None of the characters have the same goal and stakes, so that rules out a combined protagonist.

This gives us our first clue that *A Game of Thrones* is a group protagonist, and we can create a skeleton blurb for the group.

The external skeleton blurb is: The humans must choose who will sit on the throne; otherwise, the kingdoms will fall apart.

This shows us that the humans are a combined protagonist.

In summary

The following books have a single protagonist: *Fourth Wing*, *Twilight*, *The Unbroken*, *A Court of Thorns and Roses*, and *Legendborn*.

A Game of Thrones has a group protagonist.

As we study each of these novels, we'll show you how the protagonist strategy chosen by the author influenced the structure of the novels.

Perhaps you see the type of story you'd like to write in one of the six novels we're studying. Choose the same protagonist type and add that to your fantasy vault.

External Plot Skeleton Blurbs

Here you can read the skeleton blurbs for all six novels. We don't know what each author might have written. This is our view of the novels.

Fourth Wing Skeleton Blurb

External Plot Skeleton Blurb: Violet must use her intelligence to survive the Riders Quadrant; otherwise, she will die.

Twilight Skeleton Blurb

External Plot Skeleton Blurb: Bella must learn to live with her father in a new town; otherwise, her mother will not have a new life.

The Unbroken Skeleton Blurb

External: Touraine must choose the winning side in the battle between the empire, her homeland, and the Shālan; otherwise, she will die.

A Court of Thorns and Roses Skeleton Blurb

Feyre must find a way to leave Prythian; otherwise, she will never see her family again.

Legendborn Skeleton Blurb

Bree Mathes must search for the truth about her mother's death; otherwise, she won't understand her heritage and how to live among the supernatural.

Game of Thrones Skeleton Blurb

The humans must choose who will sit on the throne; otherwise, the kingdoms will fall apart.

Your Fun Task

To get the most out of this book, we highly recommend completing each fun task before moving on to the next chapter. By working through these tasks, your novel will be in a better place than when you started this book.

If you're doing the supernatural plot first, go to Chapter Five: The Supernatural Plot and follow that process, then come back here and work on the external plot.

Outlining & Editing

At this stage in the journey, the most important skeleton blurb is the one you know best. This spot is reserved for the external plot. It's time to complete your fun task.

1. Write your external plot skeleton blurb.

2. Add your external plot skeleton blurb to your fantasy vault.

Where to Next?

Writing an external skeleton blurb is a huge achievement. It means you know one plot for your story. Next, you'll create the skeleton blurb for the supernatural plot. You'll be amazed at how much these two tasks help you create the foundation for your story.

Chapter Five: The Supernatural Plot

Magic and the Mythical World

When characters wield magic or meet mythical creatures like dragons, fairies, or other non-worldly beasts, readers know they're reading a fantasy.

The supernatural story arc gives you the structure to control how to reveal the supernatural.

The supernatural is only interesting when we see how characters use and are limited by the supernatural elements. All supernatural events help or hinder the protagonist from reaching their supernatural story goal.

The supernatural must help or hinder the protagonist from reaching their supernatural story goal.

Create the Supernatural Plot Skeleton Blurb

For a fantasy novel, one of the skeleton blurbs must include the supernatural. This means there is magic and/or a mythical world.

A supernatural system refers to fantasy worlds where magic itself is a system of rules and powers, often existing alongside mythical creatures like dragons, vampires, or elves.

If you find it impossible to write a skeleton blurb that includes magic or a mythical world, the story might not be a fantasy.

From now on, when referring to the supernatural, we are referring to magic and/or mythical creatures.

We created the supernatural story arc before any subplots because without the supernatural, the story is not a fantasy.

The supernatural is only interesting when it affects major characters. When we create a supernatural skeleton blurb for a character, we use it to control the tension and pacing of the story.

The skeleton blurb for a supernatural plot is related to the protagonist because the supernatural is only interesting when it impacts characters. It looks like this:

> The protagonist must use the supernatural; otherwise, they won't achieve their story goal.

The skeleton blurb for a supernatural plot is related to the protagonist.

For example, for Violet in *Fourth Wing*, her supernatural skeleton blurb is:

> Violet must learn to control her signet; otherwise, she can't protect Navarre's borders from evil mythical creatures and all inside the borders will die.

For a group protagonist like A *Game of Thrones,* the supernatural skeleton blurb is:

> The humans must leverage the supernatural; otherwise, they can't beat the White Walkers, and they all die.

Once we have a supernatural skeleton blurb, we can create the main events for the supernatural story arc scenes.

Example Novels: Supernatural Skeleton Blurbs

The generic supernatural skeleton blurb we are looking for in each of our novels is:

A character must use the supernatural; otherwise, they won't achieve their supernatural story goal.

Fourth Wing by Rebecca Yarros

Supernatural Skeleton Blurb: Violet must learn to control her signet; otherwise, she can't protect Navarre's borders from evil mythical creatures and all inside the borders will die.

The Riders Quadrant was created for humans to bond with dragons and fight a war. This contains both magic and mythical creatures and confirms *Fourth Wing* is a fantasy novel.

Twilight Skeleton Blurb

Supernatural Plot: Bella must learn to live among vampires; otherwise, she will not find her "Happy Ever After" life with Edward.

Vampires are mythical creatures and confirm *Twilight* is a fantasy novel.

The Unbroken Skeleton Blurb

Supernatural Skeleton Blurb: Touraine must learn Shālan magic; otherwise, her people will die.

Using healing magic is key to the protagonist achieving the story goal. So much so, that if it doesn't exist, she dies. The magic confirms *The Unbroken* is a fantasy novel.

A Court of Thorns and Roses Skeleton Blurb

Supernatural Skeleton Blurb: Feyre Archeron must break an ancient curse; otherwise, she will doom her lover's world, and she will die.

An ancient wicked shadow implies there are mythical creatures in the novel. This confirms *A Court of Thorns and Roses* is a fantasy novel.

Legendborn Skeleton Blurb

Supernatural Plot: Bree must combine root magic with Legendborn magic; otherwise, the ancient ones will destroy the world.

We see there is magic in this novel, and this makes the novel fit in the fantasy genre.

A Game of Thrones Skeleton Blurb

Supernatural Plot Skeleton Blurb: The humans must leverage the supernatural; otherwise, they can't beat the White Walkers, and they all die.

This novel uses the supernatural through several characters because the protagonist is a group protagonist. Leveraging the supernatural shows us the novel is a fantasy novel.

We're going to use a character-specific skeleton blurb to illustrate one of the supernatural story arcs in this complex novel. For clarity, we've chosen one character, Daenerys Targaryen, but we could have also chosen Bran Stark for book one.

Daenerys Supernatural Plot Skeleton Blurb: Daenerys must become the mother of dragons; otherwise, she won't become the Dothraki leader and she will die.

We're including the series skeleton blurb to give you an overview of the entire story.

The A Song of Ice and Fire Series Skeleton Blurb: The humans must defeat the White Walkers; otherwise, humanity ends.

Your Fun Task

If you are starting with the supernatural, add step one and step two to your fantasy vault. Then go to the "Where to Next?" section.

Outlining & Editing

At this stage in the journey, the most important skeleton blurb is the one you know best. This spot is reserved for the supernatural plot.

Actions

1. Write your supernatural plot skeleton blurb.

2. Add your supernatural plot skeleton blurb to your fantasy vault.

Where to Next?

Where you go next depends on if you started with the supernatural skeleton blurb. In that case, go back to Chapter Four: The External Plot and write your external skeleton blurb.

When both blurbs are written, you'll create the main events for the external and supernatural plots. Either go to the next chapter: Chapter Six: Create Your External Plot Skeleton Synopsis or Chapter Seven: Create Your Supernatural Skeleton Synopsis.

Chapter Six: Create your External Plot Skeleton Synopsis

A skeleton synopsis contains a high-level description of the main events in the five story arc scenes.

We'll create the main events for the inciting incident, plot point 1, the middle plot point, plot point 2, and the climax, along with the resolution.

Main events are one-liners that capture the essence of each scene's action.

Just like you have at least two skeleton blurbs, you'll have at least two skeleton synopses. These are:

1. External plot. This is the adventure plot of the story.

2. The supernatural plot. This shows how the protagonist interacts with the magic or mythical creatures (the supernatural).

These two synopses will help you weave the storylines together.

Before we delve deeper, let's build the foundation using the external plot.

Spoiler Alert: This chapter contains the ending of the six example novels.

Fantasy External Plot Story Arc Scenes

The external plot throws a challenge at the protagonist, sends them on an adventure, causes a false victory or defeat, drives them to a low point using dark forces, and shows them achieving (or not) the story goal.

Let's look at each of these scenes in detail.

Inciting Incident: The Challenge

In the main event, your protagonist will be presented with a challenge, a problem, or an adventure to undertake.

To undertake the challenge, the protagonist will leave their ordinary world. The departure from the ordinary world can happen anywhere up to plot point 1.

The main event in a fantasy novel inciting incident often includes magic or mythical creatures. If the supernatural doesn't play a major role in the novel, it doesn't have to be in the inciting incident.

Plot Point 1: Adventure Accepted

The main event shows the character accepting the adventure and why they can't change this decision. If they can change the decision, the story is not moving forward.

Middle Plot Point: False Victory or Defeat

For a fantasy, this scene will show a false victory or defeat. The protagonist will gain new information that pushes them in a new direction.

The protagonist will face a hard moment. Their life may be at stake.

The story goal can also be in jeopardy.

Plot Point 2: Dark Forces

The protagonist will face the dark forces in your fantasy world. The dark forces may or may not be related to the supernatural elements in the story.

They will get the final piece of information they need to address the story goal in the climax scene.

They will be at the lowest point in the story. This can be physical or emotional.

Climax: External Story Goal Achieved or Not

In plot point 1, the protagonist accepts the external story goal. The climax scene shows the protagonist either achieving or not achieving the story goal in the skeleton blurb. This must be shown clearly to the reader, so they leave the story satisfied.

The following image shows the external (top row) and supernatural (bottom row) story arc functions:

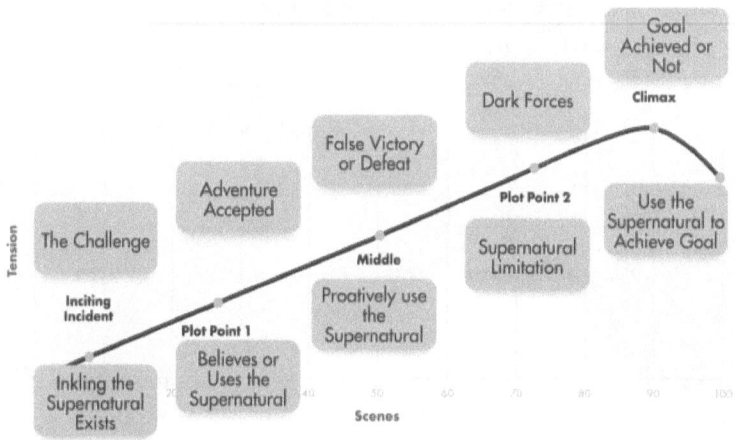

The Fantasy Novel External Plot Test

Let's look at what happens if one of the five external plot story arc scenes is missing. These scenes form the spine of your story, and every other scene works to support that story.

If there is no inciting incident, there is no story because all we're reading about is a protagonist's ordinary life.

If the protagonist is not presented with a challenge, a problem, or an adventure to undertake, the story is not a fantasy.

Plot point 1 shows the protagonist accepting the story goal. If the protagonist doesn't accept the story goal, there is no story because the protagonist does nothing.

If the protagonist doesn't accept the adventure, the story is not a fantasy.

The middle plot point shows the protagonist changing from reactive to proactive. If there is no middle plot point, the protagonist doesn't drive the story forward and cause problems, and there is no story. For a fantasy, this will be a false victory or false defeat. The protagonist will gain new information that pushes them in a new direction.

If the protagonist does not face a false victory or false defeat, the story is not a fantasy.

Plot point 2 shows the protagonist at the lowest point in the story and gives the protagonist the final piece of information they need to address the story goal. Without the new information learned in plot point 2, the protagonist cannot address the story goal. If they can never address the story goal, the story never ends. There is no story if there is no plot point 2.

If the protagonist does not face dark forces, the story is not a fantasy.

The climax scene shows whether the protagonist achieves the external story goal. If there is no climax scene where the protagonist addresses the story goal, there is no story because the story isn't over.

If the protagonist does not address the story goal in a clear manner, the story is not over.

Fourth Wing External Story Arc

External Plot: Violet must use her intelligence to fight other students in the Riders Quadrant; otherwise, she won't survive her first year as a cadet.

Fourth Wing Story Arc

Our version of a skeleton synopsis for *Fourth Wing* by Rebecca Yarros is shown below.

External Inciting Incident (The Challenge)

The inciting incident happens before the story starts. Violet's mother orders her to go to the Riders Quadrant instead of the Scribes.

External Plot Point 1 (Adventure Accepted):

Violet beats an opponent on the mat by using poison to weaken them but not kill them. She has chosen to use her intelligence to survive her first year as a cadet, thus accepting the external story goal. Violet has accepted the adventure of surviving her first year as a cadet in the Riders Quadrant.

External Middle Plot Point (False Victory or Defeat):

Violet's life is at stake because Jack intends to kill her during their match. She poisons him during the match and wins. This is a false victory because Jack still plans to kill her. She hasn't removed the threat from her life. Her story goal of using her intelligence to survive the Riders Quadrant is in jeopardy.

External Plot Point 2 (Dark Forces):

Violet faces dark forces from within the Riders Quadrant. She uses lightning to kill another cadet (Jack). This is her lowest point in the story, as she understands she can kill a person.

She learns she can use lightning. She needs the knowledge that she can kill another and that she can channel lightning in order to succeed in the climax scene.

External Climax (Goal Achieved or Not):

Violet uses both her intelligence and the supernatural to win the battle and achieve the external story goal. She lives.

Resolution:

Xaden takes Violet to a healer. She wants to let go and die, and he refuses to let this happen. Violet loves Xaden but doesn't trust him. They are bound through their dragons and must find a way to work together if they are going to succeed in book two of the series. In the resolution, Violet and Xaden do not achieve their "Happy Ever After" moment. This leads the reader to the next book in the series.

You can see this is a high-level synopsis meant to show the structure of the external plot. It does not include the supernatural or romance plots.

Twilight External Story Arc

External Plot: Bella must learn to live with her father in a new town; otherwise, her mother will not have a new life.

Inciting Incident

Before the story, Bella's mother gets married. Bella reacts to the inciting incident by moving to Forks to live with her father to help her mother's new marriage.

Plot Point 1

After an accident, Bella's mother begs her to come home, but she stays in Forks because she is consumed with Edward. She has accepted the adventure of making a new life in Forks. This occurs early in the novel, but it works because the supernatural plot is more important and the supernatural plot point 1 occurs right when it should.

Middle Plot Point

Bella tells her father that she is not going to Seattle, and so her dad offers to cancel his fishing trip. But she says there is no need. Her dad comments on how easy she is to live with. Bella is becoming proactive in creating a life in Forks. This is a false victory because Bella will be chased out of Forks by evil vampires. Her story goal of learning to live in a new town is in jeopardy.

Plot Point 2

Bella faces dark forces when the evil vampire lusts for her blood.

She leaves Forks to hide from the evil vampire. She is at a low point because she doesn't want to be separated from Edward and her father. The separation devastates her, and that is the information she needs when she achieves her story goal of living in Forks with her father.

Climax

Bella tells her mother she wants to go back to Forks. This closes off the external goal of Bella learning to live in a new town with her father. This is not the same scene as the supernatural or romance plot climax scenes.

Resolution

Bella is back in Forks and wants to become a vampire. Edward refuses to bite her and turn her into a vampire.

The Unbroken External Story Arc

External Plot: Touraine must choose the winning side in the battle between the empire, her homeland, and the Shālan; otherwise, she will die.

Inciting Incident

Touraine saves Princess Luca from an assassination.

Plot Point 1

Touraine is found guilty of murder. Luca offers her a job as her assistant. Touraine accepts. She has accepted the adventure and will try to save her people differently than originally planned.

Middle Plot Point

Touraine betrays Luca and the rebels to Cantic, thinking she is protecting the Sands. This puts her story goal in jeopardy. This is a false victory because she hasn't protected the Sands.

Plot Point 2

Touraine is no longer a Sand. She doesn't belong with Luca. Touraine fights with her mother and punches her in the jaw. This is the lowest point for Touraine because she belongs nowhere. She needs to be pushed to her absolute low to learn she would rather die fighting than kill herself.

Climax

Touraine kills Captain Rogan. She has chosen the winning side and achieved her external story goal.

Resolution

The Balladairan ships leave Qazāl, and the Brigāni and the Sands are united. Touraine is no longer part of the army.

A Court of Thorns and Roses External Story Arc

External Plot: Feyre must find a way to leave Prythian; otherwise, she will never see her family again.

Inciting Incident

Feyre leaves her home and goes with Tamlin to Prythian.

Plot Point 1

Feyre steals a knife. She promised her mother she would take care of her sisters, and she's going to keep that promise. She accepts the story goal of returning home.

Middle Plot Point

Feyre starts to realize her external story goal of returning home is the wrong goal. She's falling for Tamlin and this is weakening her resolve to go home.

Plot Point 2

Feyre faces dark forces such as the ancient wicked curse. This is her lowest point in the novel because she finds out it is her fault her friend Claire was tortured to death. If she had found a way to go home, she might have saved Claire. She also learns she must complete three tasks or die.

Climax

Feyre beats the dark forces by solving a riddle and wins the final battle. Feyre solves the riddle: The answer is love. The curse is broken, and she knows she will never leave Prythian. She has failed to achieve the external story goal.

Resolution

Feyre becomes High Fae. Feyre and Tamlin finally get to unite. She pushes the horror of killing two innocent Fae from her mind for now.

Legendborn External Story Arc

External Plot: Bree must search for the truth about her mother's death; otherwise, she won't understand her heritage and how to live among the supernatural.

Inciting Incident

The external inciting incident happens in a prologue and is also the opening image. Bree's mother dies in a car accident. Magic is present in the prologue, but Bree doesn't know it yet. Bree must face the challenge of living life without her mother.

Plot Point 1

Bree takes an oath so she can be inside of the order. She cannot turn back from this decision as it means death to her. She has accepted the adventure of finding out who killed her mother.

Middle Plot Point

Patricia (Bree's mentor) tells her she doesn't know much about her mother. Bree thinks she knows who killed her. This is a false victory because Bree is wrong.

Plot Point 2

Bree finds out her mother hid from the order and from her. By digging into her mother's past, she is undoing all the good her mother did. She learns that no matter how her mother died, she still feels incredible pain.

In the external plot point 1, Bree takes the oath so she can stay inside of the order and find out who killed her mother. In this scene, she understands this won't help her heal.

Climax

Bree discovers her mother was killed by accident. She leaves Nick, Sel, and the group. She has achieved her external goal.

Resolution

Bree now lives in a world where some support her and some don't. Her life and Nick's are in grave danger. She teams up with Sel to find Nick, putting his safety before hers.

A Game of Thrones External Story Arc

External Plot: The humans must choose who will sit on the throne; otherwise; the kingdoms will fall apart.

For this book, we've chosen to show you Eddard's story arc.

Inciting Incident

Catelyn tells Eddard that Jon, the Hand of the King, is dead. Eddard's challenge is to figure out how to help the king and protect his own family. This is the first change in the ordinary world of the kingdoms. The impact on the world is negative as this kicks off the battle for the Iron Throne.

Eddard's external challenge is how to take care of the king and his family at the same time. Eddard's reaction was to choose the king over his family. He will leave his ordinary world and live in King's Landing.

Plot Point 1

Eddard and Catelyn make a plan to protect the North if war breaks out. Eddard is going to stay in King's Landing to protect the king. Without the right king, the kingdoms will fall apart. Eddard has accepted the goal of choosing the right person to sit on the throne.

Middle Plot Point

Eddard proactively acts for the King in his absence instead of waiting for him to return. He sends knights to retaliate against Clegane for plundering land. He doesn't let Ser Loras go and makes an enemy. This is a false victory.

Plot Point 2

Varys visits Eddard in Jail. He asks Eddard to admit to treason and instruct Robb (his son) to lay down his arms. Eddard refuses. Varys warns him Sansa (his daughter) will suffer because of his actions. The Lannisters are the dark forces Eddard will have to face.

Climax

Eddard is executed by King Joffrey and has not achieved his story goal. The wrong king is sitting on the throne.

Resolution

The resolution takes place over four scenes and from four characters' POV.

Bran dreams of his father and learns Eddard is dead.

Sansa no longer wants to marry Joffrey and wants to go back to Winterfell. Joffrey takes her to see her father's head.

Tyrion's father calls him his son but only because he thinks Jaime is dead.

Robb is chosen as King of the North.

Your Fun Task

Create the skeleton synopsis using the external plot story arc scenes.

For Outlining

As a minimum, add the following main events:

Inciting Incident: The protagonist is given a challenge.

Plot Point 1: The protagonist accepts the adventure caused by the challenge. This means they are accepting the external story goal.

Middle Plot Point: The protagonist has a false victory or defeat.

Plot Point 2: The protagonist faces dark forces.

Climax: The protagonist achieves the story goal, or they don't.

Try to be as specific as possible. The foundation for your novel will be stronger when you can see the external plot clearly through the skeleton synopsis.

To create your skeleton synopsis, we recommend outlining the story arc scenes in the following order and then place them in the order they appear in your story.

Plot Point 1 Main Event

Inciting incident Main Event

Plot Point 2 Main Event

Climax Main Event

Middle Plot Point Main Event

For Editing

The skeleton synopsis is a tool used to determine if your story structure is strong before you edit the rest of the scenes in the story.

To create your skeleton synopsis, read the inciting incident, plot point 1, middle plot point, plot point 2, and climax scenes.

Describe that action in each of these scenes in one sentence. This is the main event for each scene.

Actions

Update your vault with the main events for each story arc scene. As a minimum, add the following main events:

- Inciting Incident
- Plot Point 1
- Middle Plot Point
- Plot Point 2
- Climax

Where to Next?

As with the skeleton blurbs, this depends on whether you created the main events for the external or supernatural plots first.

For those of you with the supernatural to still create, move on to Chapter Seven and create your supernatural skeleton synopsis.

And for those of you who now have both skeleton synopses created, go to Chapter Eight: Combined Skeleton Blurbs.

Chapter Seven: Create Your Supernatural Skeleton Synopsis

When we think of the supernatural as an entity in a story, we can build the story structure around the supernatural and use it to increase tension and conflict. To do this, we create a supernatural story arc.

The supernatural story arc is the journey of the protagonist in relation to the supernatural.

The supernatural story arc consists of five scenes: the inciting incident, plot point 1, the middle plot point, plot point 2, and the climax. We use the term scenes loosely, as typically, the main events for the supernatural story arc scenes are included in a scene that serves multiple purposes.

Just like the external story arc, the protagonist will be introduced to the supernatural and it will shake up their ordinary world. Somewhere around the time of the external story goal, they will also accept the use of the supernatural to achieve that goal. They'll use the supernatural reactively until they reach the middle plot point, where they begin using it with purpose. In the supernatural plot point 2, the supernatural elements will hurt or hinder the protagonist. By the climax, the protagonist knows how to use the supernatural elements to achieve the story goal.

Not all stories work exactly like this. This is a process to guide you through your story.

The Purpose of the Supernatural Story Arc Scenes

Inciting Incident

The protagonist gets an inkling the world is not as they previously understood it to be. This includes showing the reader if the story includes magic or mystical creatures.

Plot Point 1:

For an external plot, you know the main event in plot point one is accepting the story goal.

For the supernatural, this is where the protagonist accepts the goal in the supernatural blurb. This means, for the first time, they fully believe in or use the supernatural, and it is part of their life and the journey they are on.

Middle Plot Point

At the middle plot point, the protagonist starts to use the supernatural proactively. This is only sometimes needed. It can depend on the external plot's middle plot point.

Plot Point 2

The protagonist gains knowledge about or faces the first major limitation of the supernatural. This is often a painful moment for the protagonist. The pain can be internal or external. The scene often coincides with the external plot point 2.

Climax

The protagonist uses the supernatural to achieve the supernatural story goal.

The Fantasy Novel Supernatural Plot Test

Let's look at what happens if one of the five supernatural plot story arc scenes is missing. These scenes form the spine of your supernatural plot, and every other scene works to support that story.

If there is no inciting incident, the protagonist doesn't get an inkling magic exists.

If the protagonist does not interact with the supernatural, the story is not a fantasy.

In plot point 1, the protagonist fully believes in the supernatural, or they use it for the first time.

If the protagonist doesn't accept or use the supernatural to achieve the story goal, the story is not a fantasy.

At the middle plot point, the protagonist uses the supernatural proactively.

If the protagonist does not use or wish to use the supernatural proactively, the story will not be a fantasy.

In plot point 2, the protagonist gains knowledge about the supernatural faces the first major limitation of the supernatural.

If the protagonist does not face a major limitation of the supernatural, the story is not a fantasy.

In the supernatural climax, the protagonist uses the supernatural to achieve the story goal.

If the supernatural climax scene doesn't include magic or mythical creatures, the story is not a fantasy.

The main purpose of the resolution is to give the reader closure after the climax scene. The reader wants to know what the protagonist's world looks like after they have addressed the story goal.

If there is no resolution, the story may have ended, but the reader won't feel satisfied. You'll still have a story, only the reader might not read your next book.

By starting your outline or editing with the five story arc scenes and a resolution, you're guaranteed to create a strong story. When you add the fantasy guidelines, you're on your way to a fantasy readers will love.

The following shows you our version of the supernatural skeleton synopsis for each of our six books. We'll fill these in with more details later. For now, the goal is to see the high-level structure of each book.

Fourth Wing Supernatural Story Arc

This section shows the supernatural story arc for *Fourth Wing* and includes the ending. All of the following sections include the ending of the novels we have chosen.

It's important to note that each of the story arc scenes includes some element of magic. When we weave the external and supernatural plots, we'll show you how the author can place the supernatural story arc scenes near or in the external story arc scenes.

Supernatural Plot: Violet must learn to control her signet; otherwise, she can't protect Navarre's borders from evil mythical creatures and all inside the borders will die.

Supernatural Inciting Incident

Violet gets an inkling she can use her intelligence to control a dragon's behavior. As the cadets are exposed to the dragons for the first time, a dragon kills any cadet who runs. Violet understands she must stand still. The dragon faces her and breathes enough fire to heat her face but not burn her. She does not flinch. Her actions cause the dragon to move on to the next victim.

Supernatural Plot Point 1

Violet bonds with Tairn and Andarna at the Threshing ceremony. She is the first cadet to bond with two dragons. This allows her to accept the supernatural story goal of bonding with a dragon and learning to control her signet because she has bonded with two dragons, and Tairn is the most powerful dragon. Bonding is for life, so Violet cannot turn back.

Up to this point, Violet still did not believe she could live up to her mother's expectations that she could survive her first year as a cadet. Here she believes it might be possible. She needed both the external and supernatural plot point 1 events to give her this confidence.

Supernatural Middle Plot Point

Violet channels Andarna and stops time. This is Violet proactively using the supernatural to save herself. She doesn't understand how she is channeling power. You'll see later how this also forces her to make a risky decision.

Supernatural Plot Point 2

Violet uses magic to kill her enemy Jack. She creates a lightning strike that destroys the mountain Jack is standing on. With this action, she learns the power of her magic, and she'll use that power in the climax scene.

She learns magic gives her the ability to kill, but she can't control it. Using the signet depletes her and her dragon's energy, so we are shown the supernatural limitation.

The event is painful to Violet because this is the first time she's killed a person. Even though Jack was her enemy, she finds it difficult to come to terms with the killing.

Supernatural Climax

The external and supernatural climax scenes occur in the same scene. Violet controls the magic to kill venin. This is the final major change in her use of magic for book one in this series.

Violet learns that when she kills venin, the wyvern linked to that venin also dies. This is supernatural knowledge Violet needs in book two of the series.

Resolution

Xaden sits beside Violet's bed for three days while she recovers. Violet tells Xaden she still loves him, but no longer trusts him. They are bonded for life, but the relationship has changed forever.

This happens right before the closing image.

Twilight Supernatural Story Arc

Supernatural Plot: Bella must learn to live among vampires; otherwise, she will not find her "Happy Ever After" life with Edward.

Supernatural Inciting Incident

A van is inches from crushing Bella, and Edward saves her. She witnesses his superhuman strength and speed. Edward stops the oncoming van with his hands. She sees dents in the van where it hit Edward.

Bella faces the problem of figuring out how Edward could perform these extraordinary feats. She knows something is off with Edward's story, but doesn't know what that is, yet.

Bella lies for Edward, so this is also a moment that moves the romance forward.

Supernatural Plot Point 1

Bella learns about Edward's magic after he protects her from a gang of attackers and says he found her by following her scent and knew she was in trouble by reading the others' minds. Edward admits he is a vampire.

This is the supernatural plot point 1 because she has proof Edward is a vampire, and it's her first step in learning to live with vampires.

Supernatural Middle Plot Point

Bella sees Edward's true power. He shows her what he looks like in the sunlight. She decides she'll risk death to be with him.

Supernatural Plot Point 2

An evil vampire tracker desires Bella's blood, and the chase begins.

Supernatural Climax

Bella faces the evil vampire, and he beats her bloody.

This addresses the supernatural goal that Bella must learn to live among vampires. The vampires save Bella, so she has successfully learned to live with them.

Resolution

Bella is back in Forks and wants to become a vampire. Edward refuses to bite her and turn her into one.

The Unbroken Supernatural Story Arc

Supernatural Plot: Touraine must learn Shālan magic; otherwise, her people will die.

Supernatural Inciting Incident

The opening scene in this book contains the external plot's inciting incident: Touraine saves Princess Luca from an assassination attempt.

In the scene following the opening scene, Touraine executes the rebels who tried to kill Princess Luca. One of the condemned uses magic to heal a cut on Touraine's arm.

The inciting incident occurs when Touraine feels a tingling in her arm. She wonders how her wound is quickly healing on its own, so this is her first inkling that the healing magic exists.

Supernatural Plot Point 1

At her court martial, Touraine mentions Shālan magic. She shares that she thinks the Brigāni might use magic against the Balladaire. The accusers don't believe her, but the information drives Princess Luca to save her. Touraine has started the search for the healing magic. She must find the source of the magic if she is to save her people.

These events show how Touraine uses magic to save herself in this scene and foreshadow how she will use magic in the supernatural climax to save herself again.

Supernatural Middle Plot Point

Touraine reveals to Princess Luca that magic is real.

Supernatural Plot Point 2

Captain Rogan takes all the priests, priestesses, and doctors from the Temple, and Touraine runs away from the fight. The priestess's wife teaches Touraine about the tenets of the Shālan magic. The magic requires flesh to mend flesh, hence the need to eat meat. Touraine asks the priestess's wife to teach her how to pray.

They have a quiet moment together helping the sick. This will make it more painful to Touraine when Captain Rogan arrests the priestess's wife.

Supernatural Climax

Touraine gets the golden eyes and becomes a Brigāni. She kills Captain Rogan using magic.

Supernatural Resolution

The Balladairan ships leave Qazāl, and the Brigāni and the Sands are united. Touraine is no longer part of the army. This is the same scene as the external plot resolution.

A Court of Thorns and Roses Supernatural

Story Arc

Feyre Archeron must break an ancient curse; otherwise, she will doom her lover's world and she will die.

Supernatural Inciting Incident

A mythical creature bursts through the door to Feyre's home. This is her first interaction with a mythical creature (that she knows of), so it's her supernatural inciting incident. She has more than an inkling that the supernatural exists.

Supernatural Plot Point 1

Feyre comes in contact with a Bogge. The Bogge speaks to Feyre telepathically. If she looks at it, it will kill her. She is successful in not looking at the creature and understands that the supernatural is dangerous in Prythian. Lucien has shown her she must depend on other fairies if she is going to survive in this world.

Supernatural Middle Plot Point

The external, supernatural, and romance plots are all in the same scene.

This scene shows how the masks are limiting Tamlin's magic. His magic is weakening. Using magic, Tamlin shortens a table, and it takes all his energy. Feyre sees for the first time how much trouble they are in. She now knows she has to help Tamlin or he won't succeed. This is the scene where Feyre becomes proactive in her supernatural story goal.

Supernatural Plot Point 2

Feyre must kill three High Fae. This is her lowest moment in the supernatural because she kills two innocent High Fae. She also learns she can't kill Tamlin by stabbing him. This is the knowledge she needs to succeed in the climax.

Supernatural Climax

Feyre uses her intelligence to solve the riddle that breaks the supernatural curse. She is killed. Feyre achieved half of her story goal. She save's her lover's world from being doomed, but she dies.

Resolution

The fairies all bring her back to life and accept her into their lives. She becomes High Fae.

Legendborn Supernatural Story Arc

Supernatural Plot: Bree must combine root magic with Legendborn magic; otherwise, the ancient ones will destroy the world.

Supernatural Inciting Incident

In this book, the opening image contains the external inciting incident: Bree's mother is killed in a car accident.

In reaction to the external inciting incident, Bree goes to university even though her mother didn't want her to.

The supernatural inciting incident happens at the university.

Bree meets Sel, and he stops her from jumping off a cliff. She describes him as unsettlingly beautiful. The supernatural inciting incident happens when she feels his magic on her face. This is her first interaction with the supernatural.

Supernatural Plot Point 1

In the scene where Bree meets Nick, Bree runs toward magic instead of away from it. She fights Hellhounds, so she can achieve what she thinks is her story goal. She wants to find out who killed her mother. She doesn't know yet there are much larger issues at stake, and that she will be fighting the ancient ones to save the world.

Supernatural Middle Plot Point

This scene shows Bree her history through dreams. She sees Sel's ancestors. She also sees Hellhounds coming from the outer world twenty-five years ago. Bree has more power than her mentor, Patricia, and she gets proactive in sharing who Sel really is.

Supernatural Plot Point 2

Bree discovers her mother was killed by accident. She leaves Nick, Sel, and the group. She has decided she wants no more to do with magic and the supernatural.

Supernatural Climax

Bree understands who she is and removes Excalibur from the stone. Bree is Arthur's Scion and a medium.

Resolution

Bree now lives in a world where some support her and some don't. Her life and Nick's are in grave danger. She teams up with Sel to find Nick, putting his safety before hers.

A Game of Thrones Supernatural Story Arc

A Game of Thrones uses magic in a more limited way than *Fourth Wing*.

Only a few characters in *A Game of Thrones* use magic and the magic is spread throughout the books in the series. We're going to follow Daenerys. The magic is Daenerys' control and use of her dragons.

There is a strong supernatural story arc for this character. The magic is interesting because it is connected to Daenerys specifically.

Daenerys' external skeleton blurb:

Daenerys must build an army; otherwise, she can't regain her kingdom.

Her supernatural skeleton blurb:

Daenerys must control her dragons; otherwise, she can't regain her kingdom.

Supernatural Inciting Incident

A group of White Walkers kill a group of humans. This occurs in the opening scene in the novel.

Supernatural Plot Point 1

Daenerys dreams of dragons and feels warmth in their eggs. She decides to become Khaleesi instead of killing herself. She has accepted the goal.

Supernatural Middle Plot Point

Daenerys hits her brother and threatens him with death. She is becoming proactive. She hugs dragon eggs and feels her baby move in her stomach. She uses dragon eggs for strength.

Supernatural Plot Point 2

Daenerys makes a deal with Maegi to save Drogo's (her husband) life in trade for another. She doesn't know her baby's life is the chosen one. She also doesn't know Drogo's life won't be worth living, and she'll have to kill him.

Supernatural Climax

Three dragons are born. Her first step in controlling the dragons is to bring them to life by joining them on a funeral pyre. She kills Maegi in the same pyre.

Resolution

The final resolution scene is the same scene as the closing image. Daenerys becomes the leader of the Dothraki.

Your Fun Task

Create the supernatural skeleton synopsis using the supernatural story arc scenes and the resolution.

For Outlining

As a minimum, add the following main events of the supernatural story arc scenes to your story vault:

Inciting Incident: The protagonist gets an inkling the world is not as they previously understood it to be. This includes showing the reader if the story includes magic or mythical creatures.

Plot Point 1: For the first time, the protagonist fully believes in the supernatural or they use the supernatural in some way.

Middle Plot Point: The protagonist begins using the supernatural proactively.

Plot Point 2: The protagonist gains knowledge about the supernatural that they can use in the climax, or they face the first major limitation of the supernatural.

Climax: The protagonist uses a supernatural element to address both the external and supernatural story goals.

For Editing

Find the main events for each of the supernatural story arc scenes and add those to your fantasy vault.

Try to be as specific as possible. The foundation for your novel will be stronger when you can see the supernatural plot clearly through the skeleton synopsis.

Where to Next?

As with the skeleton blurbs, where you go next depends on whether you created the main events for the external or supernatural plots first.

For those of you who created the supernatural skeleton synopsis first, go back to Chapter Seven: Create Your External Plot Skeleton Synopsis.

For the rest of you, move on to the next chapter and create your combined skeleton blurb.

Chapter Eight: Combined Skeleton Blurb

So far, we've written the external and supernatural skeleton blurbs. We've created the main events for the external and supernatural story arc scenes. This gives us enough information to confidently combine the two skeleton blurbs into one. You'll update these as you work through your novel.

A combined skeleton blurb contains the goals and stakes for both the external and the supernatural plot.

The external plot and the supernatural plot must have the same protagonist.

The protagonist is the same character for both blurbs. When it's not, the blurbs cannot be combined into a single blurb. For subplots, you can create a skeleton blurb for the main character who drives that subplot.

In one sentence, a combined skeleton blurb is:

[The protagonist] must [external story goal] and [supernatural story goal]; otherwise, [external stakes] and [supernatural stakes].

This skeleton blurb represents a fantasy story.

You can now decide if every scene in your novel helps or hinders the protagonist in reaching the combined goal. Not every scene has to help or hinder the external plot and the supernatural plot goals, but they must do so for one.

Let's look at each of our books and see how to combine the external and supernatural skeleton blurbs. Some are easier to combine than others.

Example Novels: Combined Skeleton Blurbs

Fourth Wing

Violet achieves both her external and supernatural goals.

External Plot Skeleton Blurb: Violet must use her intelligence to fight other students in the Riders Quadrant; otherwise, she won't survive her first year as a cadet.

Supernatural Plot Skeleton Blurb: Violet must learn to control her signet; otherwise, she can't protect Navarre's borders from evil mythical creatures and all inside the borders will die.

Combined Skeleton Skeleton Blurb: Violet must use her intelligence and control her signet; otherwise, all those within Navarre's borders will die.

Twilight

Bella achieves both her external and supernatural goals.

External Plot Skeleton Blurb: Bella must learn to live with her father in a new town; otherwise, her mother will not have a new life.

Supernatural Plot Skeleton Blurb: Bella must learn to live among vampires; otherwise, she will not find her "Happy Ever After" life with Edward.

Combined Skeleton Blurb: Bella must learn to live in Forks with the vampires and with Edward; otherwise, her family will be destroyed, she will die, and she will not find her "Happy Ever After" moment with Edward.

The Unbroken

Touraine achieves her external goal. For the supernatural goal, she makes the first step in learning Shālan magic. The partial success is the hook to read the next book in the series.

External Skeleton Blurb: Touraine must choose the winning side in the battle between the empire, her homeland, and the Shālan; otherwise, she will die.

Supernatural Skeleton Blurb: Touraine must learn Shālan magic; otherwise, her people will die.

Combined Skeleton Blurb: Touraine must choose the winning side in the battle between the empire, her homeland, and the Shālan, and she must learn Shālan magic; otherwise, she and her people will die.

A Court of Thorns and Roses

This combined skeleton blurb is different from the other books. Feyre fails to achieve her external goal of leaving Prythian but she does see her family again. She achieves part of her supernatural goal of saving her lover's world but she dies. The reader discovers this as they read. The author knows this ahead of time.

External Plot Skeleton Blurb: Feyre Archeron must find a way to leave Prythian; otherwise, she will never see her family again.

Supernatural Plot Skeleton Blurb: Feyre must break an ancient curse; otherwise, she will doom her lover's world, and she will die.

Combined Skeleton Blurb: Feyre must break an ancient curse and be accepted by the Fairies of Prythian; otherwise, her lover's world is doomed, she will die, and she will never see her family again.

Legendborn Skeleton Blurb

Bree achieves part of her external goal. She decides to discover the truth behind her mother's death but becomes part of the magical society she wanted to destroy. She achieves her supernatural goal.

External Plot Skeleton Blurb: Bree must search for the truth about her mother's death; otherwise, she won't understand her heritage and how to live among the supernatural.

Supernatural Plot Skeleton Blurb: Bree must combine root magic with Legendborn magic; otherwise, the ancient ones will destroy the world.

Combined Skeleton Blurb: Bree must discover the truth behind her mother's death and learn to use her root and Legendborn magic without help; otherwise, the ancient ones will destroy her and the world.

A Game of Thrones Skeleton Blurb

A Game of Thrones is a complex example. We need to consider the series as well as book one in the series.

The protagonist in the A Game of Thrones series is a group protagonist: the Humans. This means the protagonist in the skeleton blurb can be any of the humans. In book one, the protagonist in the external skeleton blurb is Eddard Stark. The protagonist in the supernatural skeleton blurb is Daenerys Targaryen.

External Plot Skeleton Blurb: The humans must choose the best leader to sit on the Iron Throne; otherwise; the kingdoms will fall apart.

Eddard is the first human who tries to achieve this goal. He fails because he dies, and the weaker king (Joffrey) comes into power.

Supernatural Skeleton Blurb: Daenerys must become the mother of dragons; otherwise, she won't become the Dothraki leader, and she will die.

Daenerys succeeds because she becomes the mother of dragons. This helps humans prepare for the upcoming battle with the White Walkers.

Book One Combined Skeleton Blurb: The humans must choose the best leader to sit on the Iron Throne and build their supernatural strength; otherwise, they are not prepared for the upcoming war with the White Walkers and all humans will cease to exist.

Series Combined Skeleton Blurb: The humans must learn to work together to fight the White Walkers; otherwise, humans cease to exist.

Your Fun Task

Create your combined skeleton blurb and add it to your fantasy vault by updating the text between the square brackets:

[The protagonist] must [external story goal] and [supernatural story goal]; otherwise, [external stakes] and [supernatural stakes].

Where to Next?

You've accomplished a lot. If you've updated your fantasy vault as you've been working through this book, you'll find the next part of the process easy.

Now, you're going to take the story arc scenes for both the external supernatural plot and weave them together.

Chapter Nine: Weaving a Fantasy Story

Now that you know the main events in the external and supernatural story arc scenes, you can weave the scenes together. Weaving means you're deciding where to place the external and supernatural story arc scenes relative to each other. This is where your artistry comes in.

External Plot

The external plot is the part of the story where the protagonist wants to achieve an external goal. The external plot for a fantasy takes the protagonist on an adventure. They receive a challenge, and they address that challenge in the climax scene.

Supernatural Plot

The supernatural plot adds the unique factor that makes a fantasy hit a reader's genre expectations. This plot must show the protagonist meeting, accepting, proactively wanting, almost losing, and then addressing the supernatural story goal. Without a supernatural plot, the story is not a fantasy.

Weaving the Story Arc Scenes

You have decisions to make about whether to combine external and story arc scenes. Some writers keep the story arc scenes separate for the whole novel. Some writers choose the middle or plot point 2, and others choose the climax to bring the story arc scenes together. Whichever you choose, enjoy experimenting with the scene placement.

The external and supernatural main events can be written in one or in separate story arc scenes.

There is a maximum of ten scenes to weave.

These scenes are:

1. External Inciting Incident: The challenge is issued.
2. Supernatural Inciting Incident: The protagonist gets an inkling the supernatural exists.
3. External Plot Point 1: The protagonist accepts the adventure.
4. Supernatural Plot Point 1: The protagonist believes or uses the supernatural for the first time.
5. External Middle Plot Point: The protagonist experiences a false victory or defeat.
6. Supernatural Middle Plot Point: The protagonist uses the supernatural proactively.
7. External Plot Point 2: The protagonist faces dark forces.
8. Supernatural Plot Point 2: A supernatural limitation is shown.
9. External Climax: The protagonist does or doesn't achieve the external goal.
10. Supernatural Climax: The protagonist uses the supernatural to achieve the supernatural goal (or not).

You don't have to follow the order listed above. Your goal is to include each of the scenes in your novel. The next image shows the required story arc scenes for the external and supernatural plots. We're going to help you determine where to place these scenes relative to each other.

SECRETS TO WRITING A FANTASY

When weaving scenes, there are three guidelines. While reading these, keep in mind that you're the artist, and you get to choose if you follow the guidelines.

1. The story arc scenes occur in the same order for both plot lines: The inciting incident, plot point 1, middle plot point, plot point 2, and the climax.
2. The story arc scenes are grouped together by purpose. Both inciting incidents occur before both plot point 1 scenes. Both plot point 1 scenes occur before both middle plot point scenes. Both middle plot point scenes occur before both plot point 2 scenes, and both plot point 2 scenes occur before both climax scenes. This gives the story balance.
3. The earlier story arc scenes contain an event that makes the later story arc scenes believable.

Story Arc Weaving	
Supernatural Story Arc	**External Story Arc**
Climax	
Addresses the supernatural story goal	Addresses the external story goal
Plot Point 2	
Discovers a supernatural limitation	Faces dark forces
Middle Plot Point	
Proactively uses the supernatural	Has a false victory or defeat
Plot Point 1	
Believes in or uses the supernatural	Accepts an adventure
Inciting Incident	
Has an inkling the supernatural exists	Receives a challenge

Start Weaving

Like so many things with writing a novel, you don't have to start at the beginning. You can choose the scenes that are easiest for you to work on first. We'll start chronologically, so when it's time to use this book as a reference, it will be easier for you.

To weave the story arc scenes, decide if these main events occur in the same scene or separate scenes, then decide which event comes first. This depends on the story you're telling.

This section will help you decide on the placement of the story arc scenes and if the main events should be combined into one scene.

Inciting Incident

In the external plot main event, your protagonist will be presented with a challenge, a problem, or an adventure to undertake. The challenge is an external event that happens to the protagonist.

In the supernatural plot main event, an inkling that the supernatural exists could be internal or external to the protagonist.

This inciting incident is the least likely story arc scene to contain both the external and supernatural inciting incidents in one scene. In the six novels we examined, the external and supernatural inciting incidents happen in separate scenes. There's a good reason for this. The goals of the two plot lines have not come into play yet.

The reader needs at least one of the inciting incidents to be present in the story. In the six novels we studied, the supernatural inciting incident is always present. As these are fantasy stories, this makes sense. Creating a fantasy novel without showing the supernatural inciting incident would be like writing a romance without showing the love interests meeting.

If the external inciting incident happens before the story starts, then the event should be something that the reader understands from backstory, a flashback, or dialogue. In *Fourth Wing*, before the story starts, Violet's mother orders Violet to join the Riders Quadrant, taking power away from Violet. And in *Twilight*, Bella's mother needs to follow Bella's new stepfather around the country. Before the story starts, Bella sacrifices her own happiness in exchange for her mother's by moving to Forks to live with her father.

An inciting incident that occurs before page 1 must be shown in backstory, a flashback, or dialogue.

Plot Point 1

The main event in the external plot point 1 shows the protagonist accepting the challenge or adventure.

The main event in the supernatural plot point 1 shows the protagonist accepting the supernatural goal. This means for the first time, they fully believe in, use, or see the supernatural.

When the goal is different in the external and supernatural skeleton blurbs, consider writing these events in two scenes. For the two scenes, decide which comes first. You can always combine the events into one scene later.

Middle Plot Point

For the external plot, this scene will show a false victory or defeat. The protagonist will gain information that pushes them in a new direction.

In commercially successful novels, we often see three key events that happen in the supernatural middle plot point.

1. The protagonist usually learns something critical about the supernatural.
2. The protagonist engages with or drives the supernatural storyline forward.
3. The protagonist makes a risky decision related to the supernatural.

For both external and supernatural events, the protagonist will face a difficult moment, and their life may be at stake.

Plot Point 2

Three events happen in the external plot point 2.

1. The protagonist will face the dark forces in your fantasy world.
2. They will get the final piece of information they need to address the climax.
3. They will be at the lowest point in the story. This can be physical or emotional.

Two events happen in the supernatural plot point 2.

1. The protagonist gains knowledge about the supernatural that they can use in the climax.
2. This scene shows a limitation of the supernatural. This limitation is going to make success in the supernatural climax difficult.

You may want to write the plot point 2 events using multiple scenes. Choosing to have this written in two scenes could mean one scene shows the protagonist at their lowest point in the novel and the other gives the protagonist the final piece of information they need to address the goal in the climax.

Climax Scene

The external climax shows the protagonist either achieving or not achieving the external story goal. This must be shown clearly to the reader, so the reader leaves the story satisfied.

The supernatural climax shows the protagonist either achieving or not achieving the supernatural story goal. The protagonist must use the supernatural for the attempt.

Refer to your separate skeleton blurbs. Will the protagonist achieve both goals, only one, or neither? This helps you decide how to structure the climax. If you're writing a series, failing to achieve part of a goal is a great hook to the next novel.

The Fourth Wing: External and Supernatural Story Arcs

Let's look at *Fourth Wing* and how Rebecca Yarros wove the external and supernatural story arc scenes.

Combined Skeleton Blurb: Violet must use her intelligence and control her signet; otherwise, all those within Navarre's borders will die.

External Inciting Incident

The external inciting incident happens before the story starts. Violet's mother orders her to join the Riders Quadrant instead of the Scribe Quadrant. This scene must happen before the supernatural inciting incident. In order for Violet to interact with dragons, she must be in the Riders Quadrant.

Supernatural Inciting Incident

Xaden's dragon breathes fire on the cadets. Violet understands that if she stays still, the dragon will let her live. This is her first inkling she can influence a dragon's behavior.

External Plot Point 1

Violet uses her intelligence to beat opponents in the sparring ring. She's collected poison which she uses to weaken her opponents. She has accepted the external story goal. Tairn chooses Violet to bond with in the Threshing ceremony in the upcoming supernatural plot point 1 partly because of her intelligence. This scene occurs before the supernatural plot point 1 scene because it makes Tairn choosing Violet believable.

Supernatural Plot Point 1

Violet says the names of Tairn and Andarna at the Threshing ceremony. This means she has bonded with two dragons, and she cannot reverse this decision. If a rider leaves their dragon, they die. She must bond with a dragon, first to get a signet, and then to control it.

Supernatural Middle Plot Point

Andarna channels her power through Violet and stops time. This is a false victory because Violet doesn't know how to control the magic. This scene makes the external middle plot point believable because

Violet understands that others are intent on killing her. It's no longer an abstract concept, so she prepares to fight Jack. Because this scene makes the external middle plot point believable, it must come before that scene.

External Middle Plot Point

Violet poisons Jack with an orange. This is a false victory because she saves his life, and he goes on to try to kill her. She should have killed him.

External and Supernatural Plot Point 2

This is where the external and supernatural plot lines come together in one scene.

Violet kills Jack using lightning. She's at her lowest moment because this is the first time she's killed another person. She understands she must learn to control her lightning if she's going to survive the first year as a cadet.

External and Supernatural Climax

The climax for both plot lines occurs in the same scene. Violet uses all she's learned about the supernatural and wins the battle.

The stakes for the external and supernatural plots are different and yet the goal for each of the skeleton blurbs is addressed in the same scene.

In the climax scene she survives her first year as a cadet and learns to control her signet. Until she can control her signet she can't survive as a cadet, and until she survives as a cadet, she can't beat the evil mythical creatures and save Navarre. The two events need each other, so it makes sense that they occur in the same scene.

Here is a visual image to help you see the story. The percentages are approximate.

Fourth Wing Story Arcs

Supernatural Story Arc		External Story Arc
Climax		
Violet wins battle — 90%		90% — Violet wins battle
Plot Point 2		
Violet kills Jack using lightning — 70%		70% — Violet kills Jack using lightning
Middle Plot Point		
		58% — Violet poisons Jack
Violet stops time through dragon — 44%		
Plot Point 1		
Violet names dragons at Threshing — 35%		
		21% — Violet beats opponent with poison
Inciting Incident		
Dragon breathes fire on Violet — 10%		
		Violet ordered to Riders Quadrant before story starts

Twilight External and Supernatural Story Arcs

Combined Skeleton Blurb: Bella must learn to live in Forks with the vampires and with Edward; otherwise, her family will be destroyed, she will die, and she will not find her "Happy Ever After" moment with Edward.

External Inciting Incident

Before the story begins, Bella decides to move to Forks and live with her father to help her mother's new marriage. She wants to clear the way for her mother's happiness. This scene must happen before the supernatural inciting incident because Bella must be in Forks to meet Edward.

Supernatural Inciting Incident

Edward saves Bella from a car hitting her. She witnesses his strength, and this is part of his supernatural skills.

External Plot Point 1

After the accident, Bella's mother, Renee, begs her to come home, but Bella finds it easier to stay in Forks. She doesn't want to leave and is surprised by this. Bella needs more time to get to know Edward before she accepts the supernatural story goal of learning to live among vampires, so it makes sense this scene comes before the supernatural plot point 1. Bella must show she is willing to stay in Forks to make the supernatural plot point 1 believable.

Supernatural Plot Point 1

Bella learns about Edward's magic after he protects her from a gang of attackers and admits he found her by following her scent and knew she was in trouble by reading the others' minds. Edward admits to Bella he is a vampire. She can't turn back from this knowledge.

External Middle Plot Point

Bella tells her father that she is not going to Seattle, and so he offers to cancel his fishing trip. But she says there is no need. Her dad comments on how easy she is to live with. Bella is becoming proactive in creating a life in Forks. This scene gives Bella the ability to be alone with Edward in the supernatural middle plot point, so it must come first. The supernatural middle plot point is believable because Bella has shown her desire to stay in Forks because of Edward.

Supernatural Middle Plot Point

Bella sees Edward's true power. He shows her what he looks like in the sunlight. She decides she'll risk death to be with him.

Supernatural Plot Point 2

An evil vampire tracker desires Bella's blood. Before Edward can leave Bella in the external plot point 2 scene because he's tracking the evil vampire, the evil vampire must arrive and want Bella. Therefore, this scene must come first. This scene shows how difficult it will be to protect Bella from the other vampires and makes the external plot point 2 believable.

External Plot Point 2

Bella leaves Forks to hide from vampires. Edward leaves to track the vampire. This scene is also the romance plot point 2 because the two love interests separate and may never be together again.

Supernatural Climax

Bella faces the evil vampire. He beats her bloody and bites her. The bite will turn Bella into a vampire, and Edward saves her by removing the contaminated blood from her. This scene takes Bella away from Forks. After the climax she must decide if she will return to Forks or move to her mother's. This scene must come before the external climax so Bella has that choice to make. The external climax is believable because the reader understands why Bella is returning to Forks and not going with her mother.

External Climax

Bella tells her mother she wants to go back to Forks.

Here is a visual image to help you see the story. The percentages are approximate.

Twilight Story Arcs

Supernatural Story Arc

Climax
Bella battles vampire — 90%

Plot Point 2
Evil vampire desires Bella's blood — 76%

Middle Plot Point
Bella sees Edward's true powers and she decides to stay with him — 44%

Plot Point 1
Edward admits he is a vampire — 37%

Inciting Incident
Edward saves Bella from car crash — 11%

External Story Arc

94% Bella decides to stay in Forks

82% Bella leaves Forks

49% Bella creates distance between herself and her father

14% Bella won't leave Forks even though her mother begs her

Bella's mother gets married before story starts

The Unbroken: External and Supernatural

Story Arcs

Combined Skeleton Blurb: Touraine must choose the winning side in the battle between the empire, her homeland, and the Shālan, and she must learn Shālan magic; otherwise, she and her people will die.

External Inciting Incident

Touraine saves Princess Luca from an assassination. She is slashed by the would-be assassin. This scene must happen before the supernatural inciting incident because then Touraine will feel the magic healing her wound.

Supernatural Inciting Incident

Touraine feels tingling in the wound on her arm. In a scene leading up to the supernatural inciting incident, Touraine executes a rebel. The rebel prays for her. This makes her suspect magic might be healing the wound.

Supernatural Plot Point 1

At her court martial, Touraine mentions Shālan magic. She shares that she thinks the Brigāni might use magic against the Balladaire. The accusers don't believe her, but it's what drives Princess Luca to save her. Touraine has started the search for the healing magic. She has to find the source of the magic if she is to save her people.

In the external plot point 1, Luca offers Touraine a job. She does this because she wants access to the Shālan magic. The supernatural plot point 1 must happen before the external plot point 1; otherwise, Princess Luca has no motivation to offer Touraine a job and the external plot point 1 won't be believable.

External Plot Point 1

Touraine is found guilty of murder. Princess Luca offers her a job as her assistant. Touraine accepts because if she doesn't, she dies. There is no turning back from accepting the goal. This scene must happen before the supernatural plot point 1 to give Touraine time to trust Princess Luca.

Supernatural Middle Plot Point

Touraine tells Princess Luca the healing magic is real. Princess Luca must understand this before she is willing to make a trade with the rebels. This scene must happen before the external middle plot point, or Princess Luca has no reason to make the deal.

External Middle Plot Point

Touraine takes Princess Luca to the rebels, and they agree to trade one hundred guns for one priest.

Supernatural Plot Point 2

The priestess's wife is taken by Captain Rogan in front of Touraine. Touraine thinks it's her fault because she showed Princess Luca the magic. This supports Touraine's belief that she is part of the problem. This belief makes the external plot point 2 believable because in the external plot point 2, she is told to leave by everyone she loves or cares about. She thinks they are right to ask her to leave.

External Plot Point 2

Touraine's friend Pruett asks her to leave. The rebels ask Touraine to leave. She's not part of her army. She's not part of Princess Luca's world. She's not part of the rebels. She has her freedom but nothing else.

External Climax & Supernatural Climax

Touraine gets the golden eyes and becomes a Brigāni. She uses magic to kill Captain Rogan. He was part of the soldiers who came to stop the rebellion that the locals and the Sands were building.

The Unbroken Story Arcs

Supernatural Story Arc		External Story Arc
Climax Touraine becomes a golden-eyed Brigandi when she kills Rogan — 93%	93%	Touraine kills Rogan
Plot Point 2 Rogan takes Priestess's wife. Touraine blames herself because she showed Luca magic. — 72%	60%	Touraine is no longer part of Luca's, the rebels' or the Sands' worlds
Middle Plot Point Touraine tells Luca the magic is real — 46%	54%	Touraine betrays Luca and the rebels to Cantic thinking she has protected the Sands
Plot Point 1 Touraine intentionally mentions Shalan magic at her court martial — 21%	23%	Touraine is found guilty of murder. Touraine accepts Luca's job offer
Inciting Incident Touraine feels tingling sensation healing her wound — 4%	2%	Touraine saves Princess Luca

A Court of Thorns and Roses: External and Supernatural Story Arcs

Combined Skeleton Blurb: Feyre must break an ancient curse and be accepted by the Fairies of Prythian; otherwise, her lover's world is doomed, she will die, and she will never see her family again.

Supernatural Inciting Incident

A mythical creature bursts through the door to Feyre's home. This is her first interaction with Tamlin. He appears as a monster because he's been cursed. Before the supernatural inciting incident, Feyre killed a Fae (the wolf). The monster demands Feyre go with him as payment for the death. This happens in the same scene as the external plot inciting incident but is a separate event. This makes the external inciting incident believable because the reader is shown how powerful the monster is and how powerless Feyre is.

External Inciting Incident

Feyre agrees to go with Tamlin so he won't hurt her family. This is the last moment Feyre is in her ordinary life with her family in their home.

When external and supernatural inciting incidents occur in the same scene, you can plan scenes as separate scenes and then write them into a single scene.

Supernatural Plot Point 1

Feyre comes in contact with a Bogge and it speaks to her telepathically. This is the first time she interacts with the supernatural in such a personal manner. If she looks at it, it will kill her. She is successful in not looking at the creature and understands that the supernatural is dangerous in Prythian. She accepts the goal of getting the fairies to accept her by listening to Lucien and taking heed of his advice.

External Plot Point 1

Feyre steals a knife. She decides she made a promise to her mother to take care of her sisters and she's going to keep that promise. She accepts the story goal of returning home.

External & Supernatural Middle Plot Point

This is a powerful scene because it contains the external and supernatural middle plot points.

The external middle plot point shows she understands her relationship with Tamlin has changed. She's considering staying in Prythian instead of returning to her homeland and her family.

Using magic, Tamlin shortens a table, and it takes all his energy. Feyre sees for the first time how much trouble they are in. This shows how the masks are limiting his magic. Feyre understands what's at risk. She wants to help Tamlin break the curse but doesn't know how, and he won't tell her.

External Plot Point 2

Feyre learns her friend Claire was tortured before she died. She had given Claire's name to Rhysand and now knows she not only caused Claire's death, but she caused her to be tortured too. This is Feyre's low point in the novel. Claire's torture by Amarantha is the knowledge she needs to make the supernatural plot point 2 believable. She believes breaking the curse and ridding the world of Amarantha's power is the right thing to do.

Feyre tells Amarantha she's come to claim the one she loves (Tamlin).

Amarantha says Feyre must complete three tasks for the spell on Tamlin and the other High Fae to be broken. Amarantha also gives her a riddle, and this is the information she needs to win at the climax.

Supernatural Plot Point 2

For her third task, Feyre must stab three High Fae and kill them. She kills two innocent High Fae and discovers Tamlin is the third Fae she must kill. Because she is not High Fae yet, she can't use magic to win, and this is her limitation, but she understands Tamlin holds the magic that will prevent his death. His heart is literally made of stone and the knife can't kill him. She believes in their love. She uses the knowledge in the climax because she figures out love is the answer to the riddle.

External and Supernatural Climax

Feyre has completed the three tasks, and the fairies in the crowd are on her side now.

Amarantha says she never said when she would free them. She says she will kill Feyre unless she admits she doesn't love Tamlin. Feyre refuses to say the words.

Amarantha tortures Feyre.

Feyre solves the riddle: The answer is love, and the curse is broken. The goal in the combined skeleton blurb is achieved.

A Court of Thorns and Roses Story Arcs

Supernatural Story Arc			External Story Arc
Climax			
Feyre achieves goal and fairies accept her	93%	93%	Feyre achieves goal by solving riddle
Plot Point 2			
Feyre must stab three innocent High Fae	70%	70%	Feyre sees Claire's tortured body and knows she's responsible
Middle Plot Point			
Tamlin's magic is weakening	47%	47%	Feyre understands the risks for Tamlin
Plot Point 1			
The Bogge speaks to Feyre telepathically	22%	23%	Feyre steals a knife
Inciting Incident			
A fairy-monster arrives to take his debt	8%	9%	Feyre goes with monster to Prythian

Legendborn: External and Supernatural Story Arcs

Combined Skeleton Blurb: Bree must discover the truth behind her mother's death and learn to use her root and Legendborn magic without help; otherwise, the ancient ones will destroy her and the world.

External Inciting Incident

Bree learns her mother is dead, and she is presented with the challenge of living without her mother. This is the event that triggers Bree to go to a college her mother disapproved of. The scene has magic hidden in it, and this makes the supernatural inciting incident believable. Without this event, Bree would not be at the college to meet Sel and feel his magic, so this scene must occur before the supernatural inciting incident.

Supernatural Inciting Incident

Bree feels Sel's magic on her face. This is her first inkling that magic exists. It makes the supernatural plot point 1 believable, because Bree has felt magic and won't think the magical Hellhounds are hallucinations.

Supernatural Plot Point 1

Bree runs toward magic and fights magical hounds. Bree gets hurt and Nick takes her to the headquarters. Without this, Bree won't be in the right place to take the oath in the external plot point 1. This scene must happen before the external plot point 1.

External Plot Point 1

Bree takes an oath, so she can be part of the secret society and investigate her mother's death.

External Middle Plot Point

Patricia, Bree's mentor, tells her she doesn't know much about her mother, but Bree thinks she knows who killed her. This is a false victory because Bree is wrong. This makes the supernatural middle plot point believable because Bree needs more information about her mother and is willing to follow Patricia down her path.

Supernatural Middle Plot Point

This scene shows Bree her history through dreams. She learns root magic is to protect them from others who want to harm them and to heal them when they are hurt. She learns she can see root magic and others can't. She sees Sel's ancestors. She also sees Hellhounds entering the human world twenty-five years ago. Bree learns she has more power than Patricia. She decides to trust William with the truth about Sel and who he is.

External Plot Point 2

Bree discovers her mother hid from the order and from her. She understands she's undoing all the good her mother did and has made everything much worse. She thinks: "It hits me then, that I'd come all this way for my mother and for the truth, but the pain of existing without her, the deep searing wound in my own chest, hasn't gotten any better. It has only changed shape."

Supernatural Plot Point 2

Bree accepts Nick's offer to be his squire. The room erupts in hatred for Bree.

External Climax

The root magic and Arthur's magic come together. Vera (the oldest mother) arrives because Bree summons her from the past. Bree learns her history and that her mother died by accident. She has achieved her external story goal of finding out who killed her mother.

Bree must understand who she is before she can become Arthur's scion and a medium, so it makes sense to give Bree closure on her mother's death before she can move on. This scene must occur before the supernatural climax.

Supernatural Climax

Bree understands who she is and removes Excalibur from the stone. Bree is Arthur's Scion and a medium. She has combined root magic with Legendborn magic.

Legendborn Story Arcs

Supernatural Story Arc		External Story Arc
Climax		
Bree is Arthur's Scion and a medium — 88%		87% — Bree discovers her mother was killed by accident
Plot Point 2		
Bree accepts Nick's offer to be his squire — 78%		75% — Bree finds out her mother hid from the order
Middle Plot Point		
Bree see her history through dreams — 43%		41% — Bree learns she doesn't know much about her mother
Plot Point 1		
		21% — Bree takes oath to become part of secret society
Bree fights magical hounds — 10%		
Inciting Incident		
Bree feels Sel's magic on her face — 5%		
		1% — Bree learns her mother is dead

A Game of Thrones: External and Supernatural Story Arcs

A Game of Thrones has a group protagonist. None of the external and supernatural story arc scenes occur together. We have to look at the skeleton blurbs for book one and for the series to put the story arc scenes in context.

Book One Combined Skeleton Blurb: The humans must choose the best leader to sit on the Iron Throne and build their supernatural strength; otherwise, they are not prepared for the upcoming war with the White Walkers and all humans will cease to exist.

Series Supernatural Inciting Incident: Opening Image: A group of White Walkers kill a group of humans. This frames the series, showing the reader there is more at stake for the humans than a battle for the kingdom.

Supernatural Inciting Incident

Daenerys gets in a scalding bath, and it does not burn her, because hers is the house of dragons. Then she meets Khal Drogo. If she doesn't meet Drogo, she won't get the dragon eggs at their wedding. This scene makes the supernatural climax scene where Daenerys steps onto a funeral pyre believable because the reader is shown Daenerys can withstand extreme heat.

External Inciting Incident

Catelyn tells Eddard that Jon, the Hand of the King, is dead. This is the first change in the ordinary world of the kingdoms. The impact on the world is negative as this kicks off the battle for the Iron Throne.

Eddard's external challenge is how to take care of the king and his family at the same time. Eddard's reaction was to choose the king over his family. He will leave his ordinary world and live in King's Landing.

External Plot Point 1

Eddard talks with Littlefinger and Renly about how much debt King's Landing has. The king wants a tournament in Eddard's honor. Eddard doesn't want to spend the money.

Eddard and Catelyn make a plan to protect the North if war breaks out. Eddard is going to stay in King's Landing to protect the king. Without the right king, the kingdoms will fall apart. Eddard has accepted the goal of choosing the right person to sit on the throne.

The reaction to the plot point 1 scene shows this king is bankrupting the land, so Eddard has chosen the wrong story goal.

Supernatural Plot Point 1

Daenerys dreams of dragons and feels warmth in their eggs. She decides to become Khaleesi instead of killing herself. She has accepted the supernatural goal, and this makes the supernatural middle plot point believable because we know she's going to use the strength of her dragons to succeed.

This foreshadows the main event in the supernatural climax and makes it believable. In the climax, Daenerys decides to take her dragon eggs into the fire. And comes out the literal mother of dragons.

Supernatural Middle Plot Point

Daenerys hits her brother and threatens him with death. She hugs her dragon eggs and feels her baby move in her stomach. She uses dragon eggs for strength. Daenerys decides her baby is the true dragon and not her brother.

External Middle Plot Point

Eddard proactively acts for the King in his absence instead of waiting for him to return. He sends knights to retaliate against Clegane for plundering the land. He doesn't let Ser Loras go and has made an enemy of him. This is a false victory because Eddard has created enemies. He believes he holds power, but he doesn't. This makes the external plot point 2 believable because we understand Eddard has powerful enemies.

External Plot Point 2

Varys visits Eddard in Jail. He asks Eddard to admit to treason and instruct Robb to lay down his arms. Eddard refuses. Varys warns him Sansa, Eddard's daughter, will suffer because of his actions.

Supernatural Plot Point 2

Daenerys makes a deal with a Maegi to save Drogos' life in trade for another. The limitation is that she must trade one life for another. She cannot get the Maegi to save Drogo's life without the exchange. She doesn't know she is trading her unborn son's life. This makes the supernatural climax believable when she takes the Maegi into the fire with her.

External Climax

Eddard Stark is executed by Joffrey. Arya becomes a fugitive, and the War of the Five Kingdoms begins.

External Plot Skeleton Blurb: The humans must choose who will sit on the throne; otherwise, the kingdoms will fall apart.

Eddard failed at keeping King Robert on the throne. Joffrey succeeded in gaining the throne.

Supernatural Climax

The dragons are born, and Daenerys becomes the mother of dragons.

Daenerys' Supernatural Plot Skeleton Blurb: Daenerys must become the mother of dragons; otherwise, she won't become the Dothraki leader, and she will die.

She has succeeded in her supernatural goal.

The Series Skeleton Blurb.

Let's take this back to the series for a moment.

The series supernatural skeleton blurb is: The humans must defeat the White Walkers; otherwise, humans cease to exist.

Book one ends with a great hook. The reader understands Joffrey is the wrong king to lead the humans against the White Walkers. Daenerys is the mother of dragons and has the strength of the supernatural behind her.

The book one story is over. The kingdom is weak, and Daenerys is strong. This leads us into the second book into the series.

A Game of Thrones Story Arcs

Supernatural Story Arc　　　　**External Story Arc**

Climax
　　Dragons born.　99%

　　　　　　　　　　　　87%　Eddard executed.

Plot Point 2
　　Daenerys makes a deal　84%
　　with Maegi to save
　　　　Drogos.　　　　　　75%　Ned in jail. Arrested for
　　　　　　　　　　　　　　　　treason.

Middle Plot Point
　　　　　　　　　　　　　55%　Eddard acts for the King
　　　　　　　　　　　　　　　　in his absence.
　　She hugs dragon eggs　47%
　　and feels her baby
　　move in her stomach.

Plot Point 1
　　Daenerys dreams of　27%
　　dragons and feels
　　warmth in their eggs.
　　　　　　　　　　　　　21%　Ned decides to stay in
　　　　　　　　　　　　　　　　King's Landing to
　　　　　　　　　　　　　　　　protect the king.

Inciting Incident
　　　　　　　　　　　　　4%　Ned learns the Hand of
　　　　　　　　　　　　　　　　the King is dead.
　　White Walkers kill　1%
　　　　humans.

Example Novels: Weaving Patterns

Grouping the Story Arc Scenes

The external and supernatural inciting incidents happen before both the external and supernatural plot point 1 scenes.

The external and supernatural plot point 1 scenes happen before both the external and supernatural middle plot point scenes.

The external and supernatural middle plot point scenes happen before both the external and supernatural plot point 2 scenes.

The external and supernatural plot point 2 scenes happen before both the external and supernatural climax scenes.

The first story arc scene makes upcoming story arc scenes believable. For example, the first inciting incident (either external or supernatural) makes the next inciting incident believable.

Fourth Wing

The external and supernatural plot point 2 events occur in the same scene.

The external and supernatural climax events occur in the same scene.

Twilight

The external and supernatural middle plot point events occur in the same scene.

The external and supernatural plot point 2 events occur in the same scene.

The external and supernatural climax events do NOT occur in the same scene. This is because Bella achieves her external goal but not her supernatural goal.

A Court of Thorns and Roses

The external and supernatural middle plot point events occur in the same scene.

The external and supernatural plot point 2 events occur in the same scene.

The external and supernatural climax events occur in the same scene.

A Game of Thrones

All the external and supernatural story arc scenes occur in separate scenes. This is because the protagonist is a group protagonist.

Your Fun Task

Actions

For Outlining:

List the main events for all ten story arc scenes and place them in an order that makes sense. Add this to your fantasy vault.

Ensure the earlier story arc scenes contain an event that makes the later story arc scenes believable.

For Editing:

Find the main events for each of the ten story arc scenes and list them in order. This will show you if the scenes are in an order that supports each other.

Ensure the earlier story arc scenes contain an event that makes the later story arc scenes believable.

Checklist

Ensure the scene covers each item on this list:

- The story arc scenes occur in the same order for both plot lines.

- The story arc scenes are grouped together by purpose.

- The earlier story arc scenes contain an event that makes the later story arc scenes believable.

Where to Next?

Now that we have the story arc scenes organized, we're going to move into the world of gerne-specific patterns. These are the scenes that come before and after the story arc scenes. These are much easier to outline, write, and edit once you know the main events for both plotlines and the order you're going to place them.

PART TWO
Genre-Specific Patterns

Chapter Ten: Fantasy Genre-Specific Patterns

Genre-specific patterns are used to create scenes that readers commonly expect to see in this genre.

In part one of this book, we covered how to create the foundation for a fantasy novel. If you've done your fun tasks, you're ready to move on to the next level of detail in your story.

This section of the book covers each genre-specific scene. You'll have more scenes in your novel than we have included in this list, but these are the recommended minimum scenes needed to satisfy a fantasy reader.

You decide what scenes to include and where to place them in your novel.

You don't have to follow the order of the scenes as we've listed them. For example, we've listed the external inciting incident before the supernatural inciting incident. Your story may need the supernatural scene to come first.

You can read this section through once and follow along doing the fun tasks, or you can refer to the scene you're working on and do the fun tasks for that scene. The choice is yours.

For each scene, we'll cover:

1. The scene guidelines.

2. A summary of our example novels.
3. Patterns based on the example novels.
4. A fun task including a checklist and decisions that must be made.

Use the guidelines for the genre-specific scenes to create ideas for your story.

We've addressed the genre-specific scenes separately, but when you're writing them, they can be combined into one scene or written as multiple scenes. The key message is that these events occur in your novel if they fit your story.

As the author, you might find not every scene resonates with your story vision. That's ok. Just remember that if too many scenes are missing, the reader may feel the story is not giving them what they want. We're asking you to think about including these scenes, and as always, the decision is yours.

Every reader experiences the story differently. Our summaries of each scene in the six example novels represent our interpretation. It may differ from yours. It may differ from what the author intended. This is also true for readers of your book. What's important is that you control the story you want to tell.

As the author, you know everything about the story. The reader is building their knowledge as they read.

Your Fun Tasks for Genre-Specific Scenes

Each of the following sections includes a fun task. Your tasks will vary depending on if you're outlining, writing, or editing.

To outline, create a main event that sets the foundation for the scene. Evaluate the main event and determine if every item in the checklist can be included in the scene.

Create an outline by using the main event as a scene name. It's important to keep the name short, so it shows what the event is. At this stage, it doesn't have to show why or how the event happens.

For example, in *Fourth Wing*, the main event in the supernatural plot point 1 is: Violet names two dragons at the Threshing. That's enough for outlining. We don't need to know how she ended up at the Threshing or why she's naming two dragons instead of one yet.

The main event shows the "what", not the "how" or the "why".

This method speeds up the outlining process and gives you a clear reference to your story events.

If you're super keen, once you know the event, decide who the POV character is for the scene. Once you know that, list the POV goal for the scene. You'll record this in your fantasy vault. You may find it easier to wait and do this when you're writing the scenes. The artistic process is yours.

You can also decide if the scene moves the protagonist closer to or farther away from either the external or supernatural story goal. Record that in your fantasy vault too.

After Outlining

Once you've written a scene, check that you've included each item on the list we give you in the "Your Fun Task" section.

For structural editing, evaluate the scene to ensure all the duties are included. If not, revise the scene.

Checklist and Decisions

The "Your Fun Task" section includes a checklist and decisions that must be made during outlining or writing.

A Quick Reminder

We show the endings of the example novels. This would be a good time to read any of the books before reading our detailed analysis.

The process and the story are yours. We've shown examples of patterns in commercially successful novels. You decide what patterns to use.

Chapter Eleven: Opening Image & Opening Chapter

There are an infinite number of ways to start a novel. The opening image is the first visual a reader sees. This could be the beginning of the first chapter or a prologue. It could also be pre-text like a quote. Fantasy novels often have a quote from a fictional tomb.

In this chapter, we'll cover both the opening image and opening chapter duties. We've included these two functions together because it's important to understand the difference between them and the options you have.

Opening Image Duties

An opening image in a fantasy novel must support both the external and supernatural plots.

In a fantasy, you have two choices for showing the ordinary world, one where the ordinary world does not include the supernatural and one where it does. This depends on the story you're telling.

The opening image can but doesn't have to:

- Introduce life or death stakes.

- Show the protagonist leaving their ordinary world to go on their adventure.

- Show what the protagonist loves or cares about in this world and what they have to lose by going on the adventure.

First Chapter Duties

The first chapter of any novel has genre-agnostic duties. It's common for the first chapter to:

- Introduce the protagonist. If the protagonist is not introduced in this scene, make sure you have a good reason.

- Show the reader their first glimpse of the protagonist's ordinary world. The ordinary world is shown starting in this scene and continues through the lead-up to the inciting incident. You'll write as many scenes as you need to create the ordinary world.

- Give the reader a hint of what's at stake for the protagonist. Perhaps it's the ordinary world the protagonist is leaving, or perhaps it's their life.

- Show the tone of the story. This means if you're writing a humorous story, there must be humor in the scene. A thriller starts out thrilling. You get the idea.

- Mirror the closing image.

Considerations

Typically, the first scene shows the ordinary world in action. When the inciting incident occurs before the story starts, the ordinary world is shown in backstory early in the novel.

The length of the opening image is up to you.

Let's look at our example novels and evaluate their opening images.

Example Novels: Opening Image

Fourth Wing by Rebecca Yarros

The first text for the reader is one paragraph showing the reader that the story to come has been transcribed from an old language by a scribe at a war college. The story is to honor the dead. This is the opening image and sets the tone of the story. It shows the stakes are life or death, and the ordinary world is a war college.

The reader is then shown a quote from the *Dragon Rider's Codex*. This shows dragons and humans are intertwined in the coming story.

Chapter One introduces the protagonist (Violet Sorrengail). The story world is a school where everyone is being trained. Violet's life is at stake. Her mother has transferred her from being a scribe working in a library to being a dragon rider and fighting battles. She has trained her whole life to be a scribe and only six months to fight.

The reader is shown Violet running from her room to join the Riders Quadrant. The supernatural is already part of the ordinary world, but the reader is not shown what Violet's magic will be. The first beat ends when Violet reaches General Sorrengail's office door.

The opening image differs from some of the other books because the inciting incident happens before the story starts. This means her ordinary world is shown using backstory. When you read Chapter One in *Fourth Wing*, highlight how the author shows the ordinary world. You can use the same technique if the inciting incident in your novel occurs before the story starts. Backstory is used to show Violet's reaction to the inciting incident.

Twilight by Stephenie Meyer

The opening image is a flashforward taking the reader forward in time. It introduces the protagonist, Bella, through her thoughts. Her life is at stake as she's thinking about how she is about to die. This sets the tone as a dark fantasy. The story world includes Bella facing a hunter.

The opening image ends at the end of the flashforward.

Chapter One shows Bella moving from Arizona to Washington State. Vampires are not mentioned yet, so we are only reading the external plot and not the supernatural.

The Unbroken by C. L. Clark

The opening image in chapter one shows the protagonist, Touraine, landing in her home country as a cadet. This shows the reader the novel is a military fantasy. Touraine will leave behind life as a cadet once she accepts the story goal.

There is no mention of magic yet. The scene establishes Touraine's good friend Tibeau and her love interest Pruett. This sets up her ordinary world and the close friends whose lives she will put at risk. The reader learns what Touraine has to lose besides her own life.

The opening image ends when Touraine steps off the boat.

A Court of Thorns and Roses by Sarah J. Maas

The opening image introduces the protagonist, Feyre. She lives in a world where her family is starving, and she must hunt to feed them. If she cannot hunt, her family will starve. The stakes are all their lives.

The reader learns a little about the supernatural world, such as Faeries are dangerous and live outside the borders.

Feyre kills a wolf, and this is critical to the story. It's also the end of the opening image.

Legendborn by Tracy Deonn

The opening is a prologue. It shows the protagonist, Bree, learning about her mother's death. This is also the external inciting incident and includes magic. Bree doesn't know the magic is there yet. An experienced fantasy reader will see the magic in the scene. A reader new to fantasy might not. The author has addressed both readers, and we think that's brilliant.

The opening image ends at the end of the prologue.

A Game of Thrones by George R. R. Martin

The opening image (a prologue) shows the conflict between ice and fire. The White Walkers bring the cold and the humans want fire for warmth.

Members of the Night's Watch have journeyed outside the Wall and are about to journey back when they find dead humans. Before they can leave, all but one is killed by the White Walkers. The humans are introduced as a group protagonist.

This also functions as the series' supernatural inciting incident because the scene shakes up the ordinary world of humans by including mythical creatures: The White Walkers.

The opening image ends at the end of the prologue.

Opening Image Patterns

When we review the opening images of the six books, we see:

- Except for *Fourth Wing*, all opening images introduce the protagonist.
- All opening images show the story world. The worlds are all shown at different levels of depth.
- Four of the opening images are pre-text, a prologue, or a flashforward. *Fourth Wing* uses pre-text to set up the story world. *Twilight* uses a flashforward to set the tone of the story and foreshadow Bella's death. *Legendborn* uses a prologue to show Bree's story motivation and foreshadow magic. *A Game of Thrones* uses a prologue to set up the group protagonist for the story. Each book has a reason to use pre-text, a prologue, or a flashforward.
- All opening images show what's at stake for the protagonist or what ordinary life they are about to leave.
- The supernatural appears in some of the opening images. The number of supernatural elements in the opening image is not determined by the amount of the supernatural throughout the book.
- All opening images or first chapters show the protagonist going on a journey or already on a journey.

In *Fourth Wing*, Violet goes from a Scribe's world to the Riders Quadrant.

In *Twilight*, Bella moves from an old town to a new town with vampires. This happens in chapter one and not the flashforward.

In *The Unbroken*, Touraine moves from a journey on a boat to her homeland.

In *A Court of Thorns and Roses*, Feyre travels from her ordinary world to the land of magic and fairies.

In *Legendborn*, Bree leaves her hometown and moves to a college where magic exists.

In *A Game of Thrones*, the White Walkers are heading toward the wall. This is the new world the humans must face. The first journey will be Eddard Stark traveling to King's Landing.

- The opening images or first chapters are either a smaller version of the climax scene, or they mirror or foreshadow the climax.

In *Fourth Wing*, Violet's motivation to move from a scribe's world to the Riders Quadrant is doing the right thing for her family. In the climax, she leaves the Navarre world to join the Gryphon fighters from the rebellion. She does this to save her newfound Fourth Wing family. This changing of allegiance is the event that occurs in both scenes. The stakes in the climax are higher.

In *Twilight*, the motivation behind Bella's move from her old town to a new town is to protect her mother's new relationship. The flashforward is a misdirection of this sacrifice. In the supernatural climax, Bella is alone in the dance school with the evil vampire because she believes she is going to protect her mother from being violently killed. This escalation of stakes shows how the opening image and the supernatural climax are connected.

In *The Unbroken*, Touraine saves Princess Luca's life. In the first chapter image, saving a stranger's life, although valiant, is not as high stakes as in the climax. In the supernatural climax, Touraine uses magic to save her own life. Saving a life in the opening image foreshadows the saving of her own life.

In *A Court of Thorns and Roses*, Feyre is hunting for food and she kills a fairy, using iron, and mountain ash. She is willing to take the risks to help her family. This was not to save herself but to get more money from the pelt to help her half-starving family. In the climax, Feyre breaks the curse of a fairy, and this means that the evil fairy can now be killed. She is willing to do this to save the fairy she loves, and all the other fairies who are cursed alongside him. The opening image foreshadows the supernatural climax where the stakes have increased from the lives of her father and two sisters to all the Prythian fairies.

In *Legendborn*, Bree loses her mother to a dreadful accident. In the supernatural climax, Bree gains a new family by becoming the scion of Arthur.

In *A Game of Thrones*, the supernatural creatures kill a human in the opening image. In the supernatural climax, mythical creatures (dragons) are born to a human.

- The opening images or first chapters mirror the closing

images.

In the first chapter of *Fourth Wing*, Violet is running toward the school to begin fighting for her life. She thinks there is a good chance she'll die that day. In the closing image, Violet lives and she meets her brother. He welcomes her to the revolution and new life stretches out before her.

In the opening image of *Twilight*, Bella's life is at stake as she's thinking about how she is about to die. The closing image is a mirror to the opening image because she is with Edward, a vampire, and he won't kill her.

In the opening image of *The Unbroken*, a sandstorm is brewing. In the closing image, it's raining. In the opening image, Touraine is wearing her military uniform. In the closing image, she is barefoot. The mirror occurs because the opening image shows Touraine working with a team. In the closing image, she is alone to face the troubles to come.

In the opening image of *Legendborn*, Bree is with her father, learning about her mother's death. She is weak and lost. Nothing feels real to her. In the closing image, she is full of strength.

In the opening image of *A Court of Thorns and Roses*, Feyre is starving, in danger, and heading to a home of starvation. In the closing image, Feyre is safe in a home with an abundance of food, laughter, and love.

The closing image in *A Game of Thrones* shows Daenerys standing strong with her dragons. The opening image shows the Night Watch men in a forest unaware that the supernatural exists. The mirror exists because we are shown people who don't know the supernatural exists and it ends with people knowing the supernatural exists.

Your Fun Task

Actions

For Outlining:

Create the main event for the opening image and add it to your fantasy vault. You may find the main opening image is easier to determine after you've outlined the novel.

For Editing:

In one to two sentences, summarize the main event for the opening image and add it to your fantasy vault. Since you're at the editing phase, now is the time to make sure the opening image fits the novel that you wrote.

Decisions

While outlining, make the following decisions and add them to your fantasy vault:

- Will the supernatural be included in the opening image?
- Does the protagonist know about the supernatural?

- Will the opening image be pretext, a prologue, flashforward, or chapter?

- Will the opening image be a scene on its own or within another scene?

Checklist

○ Introduce the protagonist.

○ Show the ordinary world.

○ Show what's at stake for the protagonist or what they are leaving behind in their ordinary world.

○ Introduce the journey the protagonist is going on (this can also be in chapter one).

Chapter Twelve: Lead-Up to the External Inciting Incident

This is the last moment the protagonist lives in their ordinary world. After the upcoming inciting incident, the protagonist cannot return to their ordinary world because something has changed that world forever.

There may be multiple scenes between the opening image and the lead-up to the external inciting incident. Each story has its own needs, and you'll discover these needs as you go through the genre-specific scenes.

The main event in this scene must show the reader why the story goal in the skeleton blurb is important to the protagonist.

This scene shows the protagonist's motivation to accept the external story goal.

Fantasy Genre-Specific Duties

The event must be related to the external story goal and not just the supernatural goal.

This scene can come before, after, or in the supernatural inciting incident. We're making sure the main event is included. You'll write the scenes in a way that works for your story.

Example Novels: Lead-Up to the External Inciting Incident

Fourth Wing by Rebecca Yarros

The external inciting incident occurs before page one, meaning this scene does too. We learn from backstory that before the inciting incident, Violet intended to be a scribe. That's enough for the reader to understand how difficult it will be for her to transition from a scribe to a dragon rider. She's going from spending her time in a library to spending her time at war riding a dragon.

Violet follows the orders of her mother, the general. Her external reason for achieving the story goal of surviving the Riders Quadrant is to live. She feels powerless against her mother and feels she must accept the story goal.

Twilight by Stephenie Meyer

The external inciting incident happens before the story starts, so this scene does too.

In the external inciting incident, Bella decided to move to Forks and live with her father to help her mother's new marriage. Her motivation to move is helping her mother be happy.

The Unbroken by C. L. Clark

Touraine disembarks from a ship and notices suspicious behavior. She sees Princess Luca for the first time. This is the last moment

Touraine won't be torn between life as a cadet and life with Princess Luca. She's in her ordinary world performing as a soldier.

This scene shows Touraine's motivation to succeed as a soldier and to choose the winning side. Touraine's care for others shows why her story goal of stopping the rebellion is important.

A Court of Thorns and Roses by Sarah J. Maas

Feyre is still working toward her goal in her ordinary life. For the moment, she can't see past the strain of feeding her family, so she sells the wolf pelt in the local market. This scene shows Feyre's motivation to feed her family.

She's given a warning to be careful in the forest because faes are slipping through the wall. This is a hint of the supernatural to come and foreshadows the arrival of a fae in the supernatural inciting incident.

This scene makes the external inciting incident (Feyre leaves with the fae) believable.

Legendborn by Tracy Deonn

The lead-up to the inciting incident is told in backstory. The reader learns about Bree's fight with her mother right before her mother dies. The backstory shows Bree's motivation to find out who killed her mother. Without this told in backstory, the external goal is not believable.

A Game of Thrones by George R. R. Martin

This event occurs in the first half of the external inciting incident scene where Catelyn tells Eddard that the Hand of the King is dead. Eddard believes the king must be safe for his own family to be safe. This scene shows Catelyn and Eddard (Ned) talking about their children and sets up the stakes for both Starks. They have a family to lose if things go wrong.

Lead-Up to the External Inciting Incident Patterns

There is much we can learn from these examples.

Fourth Wing and Twilight have external inciting incidents that occur before the story starts. This means the lead-up to the external inciting incident also happens before the story starts and illustrates the flexibility of the story arc scenes.

Legendborn shows the external inciting incident in a prologue, which also means the lead-up to the external inciting incident occurs before the story starts.

All six novels show why the story goal stated in the external skeleton blurb is important to the protagonist. This illustrates why we believe the character growth scenes are the lead-up and reaction scenes to story arc scenes. You'll see this pattern build throughout each of the example novels.

The following are the protagonist's external reasons for achieving their story goals:

> Violet's is to live.
>
> Bella's is to help her mother's new marriage succeed.
>
> Touraine's is to live.

Feyre's is to keep her family from starving to death.

Bree's is to ease her guilt about fighting with her mother right before she died.

Eddard's is to protect his family.

Your Fun Task

Actions

For Outlining:

Create the main event for the lead-up to the external inciting incident and add it to your fantasy vault.

For Editing:

In one to two sentences, summarize the main event for the lead-up to the external inciting incident and add it to your fantasy vault.

Decision

While outlining, make the following decision and add it to your fantasy vault:

- Will this scene come before, after, or be part of the supernatural inciting incident?

Checklist

○ Show the main event is related to the external story goal.

o Show the protagonist's motivation to accept the external story goal.

Chapter Thirteen: External Inciting Incident

The Five Duties of All Story Arc Scenes

For all genres, it's common for the five story arc scenes (the inciting incident, plot point 1, middle plot point, plot point 2 and the climax) to have the following duties in common:

1. Contains new information about the story goal.
2. Changes the story direction.
3. Raises the stakes.
4. Is full of tension (even in the quieter scenes).
5. Is written in the protagonist's POV.
6. Causes the protagonist to react to the action.

An external inciting incident can happen before the story starts. In this case, the key information in duties will be shown in backstory or a flashback.

Fantasy Genre-Specific Duties

The protagonist will be presented with a challenge, a problem, or an adventure to undertake. This is the disruption in their world.

If the protagonist is not presented with a challenge, a problem, or an adventure to undertake, the story is not a fantasy.

To undertake the challenge, the protagonist may physically leave their ordinary world. The departure can happen anywhere up to plot point 1.

An external inciting incident in a fantasy novel has genre-specific duties. The main event must be related to the story goal stated in the external plot skeleton blurb.

If the external inciting incident happens before the story starts, the opening image happens after the inciting incident and after the lead-up to the inciting incident. These two scenes must be told using backstory or a flashback.

Let's see how our example novels are doing.

Example Novels: External Inciting Incident

Fourth Wing by Rebecca Yarros

The external inciting incident happens before the story starts. Violet's mother orders her to go to the Riders Quadrant instead of the Scribes Quadrant. This information is given through backstory early in the novel.

Violet's reaction is to train for fighting. Her external challenge is to get strong enough to fight others during her first year as a cadet.

Violet must face the challenge of becoming a dragon rider and must leave her ordinary world as a scribe to do that.

This sets up the external story goal: Violet must use her intelligence to fight other students in the Riders Quadrant.

Twilight by Stephenie Meyer

Before the story, Bella's mother gets married. This prompts Bella to move and Forks to live with her father to help her mother's new marriage. Her goal is to find a way to live with her father so she can give her mother the space to be happy. We learn this through backstory.

Bella's reaction to moving is to try to please her father.

Her external challenge is to figure out how to live with her father.

She leaves her ordinary world with her mother to start an adventure living with her father.

This sets up the external story goal: Bella must learn to live with her father in a new town.

The Unbroken by C. L. Clark

A rebel attempts to assassinate Princess Luca, and Touraine saves Luca's life.

This is the moment when Touraine's life changes because she stands out from the other Sands. It leads her to meet Luca and is a step toward choosing the winning side in the battle between the empire, her homeland, and the Shālan.

Touraine must face the challenge of standing out from the others, even though it's dangerous.

Her reaction is to be proud of saving Princess Luca's life. Her external challenge is to survive now that she's made herself stand out from the other soldiers.

SECRETS TO WRITING A FANTASY

Unaware she is leaving the world of a cadet and entering the world of royalty, Touraine begins her adventure in her new world.

This sets up the external story goal: Touraine must choose the winning side in the battle between the empire, her homeland, and the Shālan.

A Court of Thorns and Roses by Sarah J. Maas

The lead-up to this scene was the last moment Feyre existed in her ordinary life with her family in their home. A monster (fae) comes to collect the debt. Feyre killed a fae (the wolf), so she must go with the monster in exchange for the wolf's life.

In the external inciting incident, Feyre accepts she must go with the monster without fighting him. Her external challenge is to survive living in Prythian.

The reader learns an important magic rule: Fairies can't lie to humans.

This scene has double duty because it is also the lead-up to the supernatural inciting incident.

This sets up the external story goal: Feyre must find a way to leave Prythian.

Legendborn by Tracy Deonn

The external inciting incident happens in a prologue and is also the opening image. Bree's mother dies in a car accident.

Magic is present in the prologue, but Bree doesn't know it yet. Bree must face the challenge of living life without her mother. This shows us this scene is not a supernatural inciting incident because Bree doesn't get an inkling that magic exists.

Bree will leave her ordinary world and go to a college her mother didn't approve of.

This sets up the external story goal: Bree must decide between discovering who killed her mother or taking down a magical society.

A Game of Thrones by George R. R. Martin

Catelyn tells Eddard that Jon, the Hand of the King, is dead. Eddard's challenge is to figure out how to help the king and protect his family. This is the first change in the ordinary world of the kingdoms. The impact on the world is negative as this kicks off the battle for the Iron Throne.

Eddard's external challenge is how to take care of the king and his family at the same time. His reaction was to choose the king over his family. He will leave his ordinary world and live in King's Landing.

This sets up the external story goal: The humans must choose the best leader to sit on the Iron Throne.

External Inciting Incident Patterns

Five of the six novels have the supernatural in the external inciting incident. In *The Unbroken*, magic is a smaller part of the story, so it works that magic is not part of the external inciting incident.

Fourth Wing and *Twilight* show an external inciting incident that occurs before the story starts and is told in backstory.

Each scene is written from the protagonist's point of view.

SECRETS TO WRITING A FANTASY

Each scene sets up the story goal stated in the relevant skeleton blurb.

Each protagonist is presented with a challenge, a problem, or an adventure to undertake.

> Violet must learn to become a dragon rider.
>
> Bella must figure out how to live with her father in Forks.
>
> Touraine must survive after she's made herself stand out from the other soldiers.
>
> Feyre must survive living in Prythian as a human.
>
> Bree must learn how to live without her mother.
>
> Eddard must figure out how to help the king and protect his family.

All novels show the protagonist leaving their ordinary world and going on a journey or setting up the story so the protagonist will leave their ordinary world.

> Violet moves from the Scribes Quadrant to the Riders Quadrant.
>
> Bella moves from Phoenix to Forks.
>
> Touraine leaves her life on a ship to life on land.
>
> Feyre leaves her home and travels to Prythian.
>
> Bree leaves her home and goes to college.
>
> Eddard leaves the North and goes to King's Landing.

You can see why these books hooked readers and kept them reading.

Your Fun Task

Actions

For Outlining:

Create the main event for the external inciting incident and add it to your fantasy vault.

For Editing:

In one to two sentences, summarize the main event for the external inciting incident and add it to your fantasy vault.

Decisions

While outlining, make the following decisions and add them to your fantasy vault:

- Will the supernatural be included in the external inciting incident?

- Does the protagonist physically leave their ordinary world?

- Will the external exciting incident happen before the story starts or after?

Checklist

○ Contains new information about the story goal.

- Changes the story direction.

- Raises the stakes.

- Is full of tension (even in the quieter scenes).

- Is written in the protagonist's POV.

- Causes the protagonist to react to the action. The reaction is the start of the protagonist's journey.

- Is early in the story or happens before the story starts.

- Is related to the story goal stated in the external plot skeleton blurb.

- Presents the protagonist with a challenge, a problem, or an adventure to undertake.

Chapter Fourteen: Reaction to the External Inciting Incident

This scene shows how the inciting incident impacts the protagonist. Reaction scenes give readers time to connect with a character, and to do that, they need to see how the character reacts to an event that changes their ordinary world.

This might be the first scene where a protagonist is shown reacting to a main event in a story arc scene. That depends on whether the external or the supernatural inciting incident comes first in your story.

Use this scene to reveal the protagonist's current personality and foreshadow potential growth areas or a stubborn resistance to change. You can hint at their potential for transformation. Any character trait should help or hinder the protagonist when they try to achieve the story goal.

The reaction to the external inciting incident reveals the protagonist's traits and can foreshadow their growth.

The inciting incident is early in the story, so if the protagonist initially grows or changes because of the main event in the inciting incident, it won't be by much.

Example Novels: Reaction to External Inciting Incident

Fourth Wing by Rebecca Yarros

The reaction to the external inciting incident occurs before the story opens. Through backstory, the reader learns Violet trained for six months to learn to fight, showing she is willing to try. This is a trait she will need in order to survive.

Twilight by Stephenie Meyer

Bella tries her best to be happy about moving to Forks and living with her father. This shows Bella is willing to adapt to a new environment, and this is a trait she will need if she is to live with vampires.

The Unbroken by C. L. Clark

In the external inciting incident, Touraine saves Princess Luca's life. In this reaction scene, she executes two people on behalf of Princess Luca even though she doesn't want to. This shows she obeys orders. This is a trait she'll change throughout the story, or she won't achieve her story goal.

There is magic in the scene. The woman about to be executed by Touraine heals Touraine's wound. This reaction scene is also the supernatural inciting incident. Touraine doesn't understand how she healed. This starts the supernatural elements of the novel.

A Court of Thorns and Roses by Sarah J. Maas

In the external inciting incident, Feyre left with the fae. In this reaction scene, he gives her a white horse to ride during the journey to Prythian. During this journey, she thinks about what she knows of Prythian. She knows that humans who go there don't return. This shows us Feyre is willing to sacrifice herself for others.

The fae uses magic to control Feyre. We assume the fae wants to hide the journey from her, so she can't find her way back to her home. This shows how little power she has in the presence of a fae.

Legendborn by Tracy Deonn

Bree goes to university even though her mother didn't want her to. We learn this in backstory three months after the death of Bree's mom. We don't know why Bree's mother didn't want her to attend this particular school. This shows Bree is stubborn and does what she feels is right for herself.

A Game of Thrones by George R. R. Martin

In the external inciting incident, Eddard learns that Jon, the Hand of the King, is dead. Eddard's external challenge is how to take care of the king and his family at the same time. Eddard's reaction was to choose the king over his family. This shows Eddard is loyal to the crown over his family.

Reaction to the External Inciting Incident Patterns

All six novels show a personality trait of the protagonist.

> Violet trained for six months to learn to fight, showing she is willing to try.

Bella is willing to adapt to a new environment.

Touraine obeys orders at all costs.

Feyre is willing to sacrifice herself for others.

Bree is stubborn and does what she feels is right for herself.

Eddard is loyal to the crown over his family.

Your Fun Task

Actions

For Outlining:

Create the main event for the reaction to the external inciting incident and add it to your fantasy vault.

For Editing:

In one to two sentences, summarize the main event for the reaction to the external inciting incident and add it to your fantasy vault.

Decisions

While outlining, make the following decisions and add them to your fantasy vault:

- What personality trait will the scene show?

- Will the scene foreshadow growth?

Checklist

○ Show the protagonist's reaction to the main event in the external inciting incident. Specifically, to the challenge, problem, or adventure.

○ Reveal personality traits that will help or hinder the protagonist when they try to achieve the external story goal.

Chapter Fifteen: Lead-Up to the Supernatural Inciting Incident

The purpose of this scene is to show the protagonist's lack of power in their ordinary world.

This is the last moment the protagonist lives in a world where they don't know the supernatural exists or haven't been able to use it yet.

Here is an opportunity to show character motivation for the protagonist to gain power by using the supernatural elements throughout the story.

This scene also makes the main event in the supernatural inciting incident believable and tense. The event must be related to the supernatural skeleton blurb goal and not just the external skeleton blurb goal.

You can place this scene before, after, or in the external inciting incident scene. We're making sure the main event is included in the story. You decide where it will be placed.

Example Novels: Lead-Up to Supernatural Inciting Incident

Fourth Wing by Rebecca Yarros

Xaden transfers Violet to his wing, Fourth Wing. This gives him control over her. He can punish her whenever he wants. She has no power to fight him yet. This makes her bravery in the upcoming supernatural inciting incident stronger.

Twilight by Stephenie Meyer

Bella sees Edward in the cafeteria. She is drawn to him but doesn't know why. She has no power to control her reaction to him.

The Unbroken by C. L. Clark

General Cantic gives Touraine the honor of executing the prisoners who tried to kill Princess Luca. She is powerless and accepts the honor with little emotion because it is her duty. This emotion is contrasted in the supernatural inciting incident where she has difficulty executing people who share her history. She has no power to refuse the general.

A Court of Thorns and Roses by Sarah J. Maas

Feyre meets a woman in the market and sells her the wolf pelt. The woman warns Feyre to be careful. She tells her the High Fae have been slipping into the woods. Feyre has no power to fight a fae and the knowledge scares her. This makes the supernatural inciting incident believable.

Legendborn by Tracy Deonn

Bree breaks school rules and goes to a party that is out of bounds. At the party, other students are jumping off a cliff. She's alone and staring at the cliff. Sel appears and warns her not to jump. This is their first meeting. This makes the supernatural inciting incident believable because she is afraid of Sel. She has no power to fight him yet.

A Game of Thrones by George R. R. Martin

Daenerys submerges in a scalding bath and it does not burn her, because hers is the house of dragons. She meets Khal Drogo and doesn't want to marry him, but she must. She has no power to refuse the marriage.

Lead-Up to Supernatural Inciting Incident Patterns

All six novels show the protagonist's lack of power by putting them in a vulnerable or powerless situation.

> Violet is transferred to Xaden's wing. He has power over her.
>
> Bree can't control her reaction to Edward and is powerless to resist him.
>
> Touraine must execute the prisoners. She has no power to refuse.
>
> Feyre has no power to fight the fae who are invading their land.
>
> Bree has no power to fight Sel and his magic.
>
> Daenerys is being sold to Khal Drogo and can't refuse. She is at his mercy.

Each scene shows why the protagonist needs the supernatural to achieve their combined story goal. They are not strong enough on their own to achieve either goal.

Without the supernatural, Violet can't survive her first year in the Riders Quadrant.

Bella needs to survive with Edward, or she can't stay in Forks and have her "Happy Ever After" moment with him.

Touraine needs Shālan magic if she is to have control over her life.

Feyre needs fairy magic if she is going to survive in Prythian and save her family.

Bree needs her own magic in order to survive.

Daenerys needs the power of dragons in order to survive.

Your Fun Task

Actions

For Outlining:

Create the main event for the lead-up to the supernatural inciting incident and add it to your fantasy vault.

For Editing:

In one to two sentences, summarize the main event for the lead-up to the supernatural inciting incident and add it to your fantasy vault.

Decisions

- Will this scene occur before, after, or in the external inciting incident scene?

- How will you show the protagonist's lack of power?

Checklist

○ Show the protagonist's lack of power by putting them in a vulnerable situation.

○ Show why the protagonist needs the supernatural to achieve their external story goal.

Chapter Sixteen: Supernatural Inciting Incident

In this scene, the protagonist gets an inkling that the supernatural exists, or they know it exists and they get a hint they can use it. The reader can be shown if the story includes magic or mythical creatures, such as vampires, dragons, or fairies.

This scene can be placed anywhere from the opening image up to the external plot point 1. If it's placed after the external plot point 1, where the protagonist accepts the adventure, the protagonist won't know their adventure includes magic or mythical creatures until this scene occurs.

The reader will expect this scene to play out on the page. We strongly recommend this scene doesn't happen before the story starts. That works for the external inciting incident but not this scene.

Example Novels: Supernatural Inciting Incident

Fourth Wing by Rebecca Yarros

Violet gets an inkling she can use her intelligence to control a dragon's behavior. As the cadets are exposed to the dragons for the first time, a dragon kills any cadet who runs. Violet understands she must stand still. The dragon faces her and breathes enough fire to heat her face but not burn her. She does not flinch. Her actions cause the dragon to move on to the next victim.

Violet shows herself that she can control a dragon's behavior through her own behavior. This is her first inkling she can control or use the supernatural, which lines up with her supernatural goal of controlling her signet.

Twilight by Stephenie Meyer

A van careens toward Bella and is about to crush her. Bella sees Edward stop the oncoming van with his hands. She also sees dents in the van where it hit Edward. She witnesses his strength, and this is part of his supernatural powers.

Bella is desperate to learn how Edward performed these extraordinary feats. She knows something is off with his story but doesn't know what that is, yet. This is her inkling the supernatural exists. Bella's goal in the supernatural skeleton blurb is to learn to live among vampires. First, she must discover that vampires exist.

The Unbroken by C. L. Clark

Touraine must execute the rebels on behalf of Princess Luca. A woman about to be executed heals Touraine's wound. Touraine doesn't understand how the wound healed. This gives Touraine an inkling the supernatural exists and starts the supernatural storyline. Touraine's goal in the supernatural skeleton blurb is to learn Shālan magic.

This event occurs in the same scene as the reaction to the external inciting incident.

A Court of Thorns and Roses by Sarah J. Maas

A mythical creature bursts through the door into Feyre's home. Although she doesn't know it, this is her first interaction with Tamlin. She sees this as her first interaction with the supernatural.

Feyre's supernatural goal is to break an ancient curse that is hurting her lover. To do so, she must meet Tamlin.

This event occurs in the same scene as the external plot inciting incident.

Legendborn by Tracy Deonn

Bree feels Sel's magic on her face. This is the first time she knowingly interacts with magic. Note that Bree sees magic in the opening image, but she does not get an inkling the supernatural exists, so that scene doesn't work as her supernatural inciting incident.

Bree's goal in the supernatural skeleton blurb is to combine root magic with Legendborn magic. This is her first interaction with any type of magic.

A Game of Thrones by George R. R. Martin

The opening image (a prologue) shows the conflict between ice and fire. This is the series' supernatural inciting incident because it kicks off the story between the humans and the White Walkers. The White Walkers' magic kills all but one human.

The humans' supernatural goal is they must leverage the supernatural.

For book one, the supernatural inciting incident is when Daenerys gets in a scalding bath and it does not burn her, because hers is the house of dragons. Then she meets Khal Drogo. If she doesn't meet Drogo, she won't get the dragon eggs at their wedding.

Supernatural Inciting Incident Patterns

Let's summarize where the supernatural inciting incident happens in our six novels.

All novels show the supernatural inciting incident happening. It does not occur before the story starts, in summary, in backstory, or in a flashback. This scene is shown in action.

Both the external and supernatural inciting incidents occur before the external and supernatural plot point 1 scenes. This little piece of knowledge helps you check that you've woven the scenes in the strongest way.

Both inciting incident scenes occur before the first plot point 1 scene.

All scenes show the protagonists interacting with or seeing the supernatural. Notice the events happen to the protagonist.

> Dragons threaten the cadets including Violet. She shows herself she can control a dragon through her own behavior.
>
> Bella sees Edward stop the oncoming van with his hands.
>
> The woman about to be executed by Touraine heals Touraine's wound.
>
> A mythical creature burst through the door to Feyre's home.

Bree feels Sel's magic on her face.

Daenerys is not burned by a scalding bath, because hers is the house of dragons.

All the supernatural inciting incidents occur near an external story arc scene, and this strengthens both scenes. The supernatural inciting incidents happen as early as the opening image and as late as the lead-up to plot point 1.

For the novels, the supernatural inciting incident is placed as follows:

The Unbroken and *Legendborn*: in the same scene as the reaction to the external inciting incident.

In *A Court of Thorns and Roses*: right before the external inciting incident.

In *Twilight*: right after the external inciting incident.

A Game of Thrones: in the opening image. This is the earliest placement.

Fourth Wing: immediately before the external plot point 1. This is the latest placement.

This reminds us that the placement of scenes in the outline is flexible. You decide what's best for your story.

Your Fun Task

Actions

For Outlining:

Create the main event for the supernatural inciting incident and add it to your fantasy vault.

For Editing:

In one to two sentences, summarize the main event for the supernatural inciting incident and add it to your fantasy vault.

Decision

While outlining, make the following decision and add it to your fantasy vault:

- Where will this scene be in your story relative to the external inciting incident?

Checklist

- Shown in action.

- Occurs before both the external and supernatural plot point 1 scenes.

- Shows the protagonist interacting with the supernatural.

- Is full of tension (even in the quieter scenes).

- Causes the protagonist to react to the action.

- Relates to the story goal stated in the supernatural skeleton blurb.

Chapter Seventeen: Reaction to the Supernatural Inciting Incident

In the inciting incident, when your protagonist gets an inkling that the supernatural exists, or they know the supernatural exists and they get a hint they can use the supernatural, they must react to this event.

Their reaction can be positive or negative. It can be full of action, an internal reaction, or both. This is another moment where you connect your readers to your character by showing who they are now and hinting at how they will change.

This scene shows the internal growth the protagonist needs in order to achieve the story goal. The protagonist internalizes a misbelief about their abilities, and the reader is shown what the protagonist must learn to fully believe in the supernatural.

Example Novels: Reaction to the Supernatural Inciting Incident

Fourth Wing by Rebecca Yarros

As the names of dead cadets are read, Violet realizes that everyone around her knows they could die at any time. Violet still hasn't accepted the goal of surviving the year, but she is acutely aware she might not. Even though the supernatural inciting incident showed her she could control a dragon's behavior using her intelligence, she doesn't believe this yet. She must learn to trust her abilities, or she won't achieve the combined story goal.

Twilight by Stephenie Meyer

After Edward stops the van from hitting Bella, she can't come up with a reason other than insanity for how Edward saved her. She doesn't believe in the supernatural yet.

Bella pressures Edward to tell her how he stopped the van. He refuses to answer. She gets angry and becomes determined to find out. This shows she's stubborn which is a trait that puts her in danger later in the novel. In the climax, she is determined to fight by herself. She doesn't learn from this scene, and that's why she fails to achieve her supernatural goal.

The Unbroken by C. L. Clark

Touraine tries to convince herself magic doesn't exist and there are no gods. She resists the idea that magic healed her wound. This shows she must open herself to the existence of healing magic. If she doesn't, she won't achieve the story goal. We'll see in the climax that she changes her belief about magic and the gods.

A Court of Thorns and Roses by Sarah J. Maas

The supernatural inciting incident occurs before the external inciting incident.

The fae arrives at Feyre's door (supernatural inciting incident).

Feyre leaves with the fae (external inciting incident).

The reaction to the supernatural inciting incident occurs between these two events. Feyre understands she's powerless to fight the fae. She knows if she tries, she'll endanger her family. She relents and tells the fae she will go to Prythian without a fight. This shows she will sacrifice herself for others and foreshadows the danger to come. It's a trait readers love.

Legendborn by Tracy Deonn

Bree hides from Sel that she can feel his magic on her skin. This shows an instinct to protect herself.

She runs to help Alice (her friend) and ignores all thoughts about Sel. This is the action part of the scene. When she sees magic shimmering, she realizes no one else can see it, and she blames the sight on her grief. This shows where Bree is emotionally, and part of her growth will be learning to trust herself. She can't achieve the story goal without this trust.

A Game of Thrones by George R. R. Martin

Daenerys meets Drogo, and her instinct is to run and hide. She doesn't believe the power she showed by getting into a scalding bath is real. She has not accepted she has the power of dragons in her and can't achieve the story goal without this acceptance.

Reaction to the Supernatural Inciting Incident Patterns

In all six novels, the protagonist doesn't believe in the supernatural yet.

Violet doesn't believe in her abilities to control the supernatural.

    Bella can't understand how Edward saved her.

    Touraine resists the idea that magic healed her wound.

Feyre believes she has no power against a Fae.

When Bree sees the magic shimmering, she realizes no one else can see it, and she blames the sight on her grief.

Daenerys doesn't believe she has the power of dragons.

The protagonists all need internal growth that will enable them to believe the supernatural can help them achieve their goal.

Violet must learn to trust her abilities.

Bella must learn to not be so stubborn.

Touraine must learn to be open-minded to the possibility of healing magic.

Feyre must learn not to be so quick to sacrifice herself.

Bree must learn to trust what she sees.

Daenerys must learn she has power.

Your Fun Task

Actions

For Outlining:

Create the main event for the reaction to the supernatural inciting incident and add it to your fantasy vault.

For Editing:

SECRETS TO WRITING A FANTASY

In one to two sentences, summarize the main event for the reaction to the supernatural inciting incident and add it to your fantasy vault.

Decisions

While outlining, make the following decisions and add them to your fantasy vault:

- Will the protagonist's reaction to the supernatural inciting incident be positive or negative?

- What does the protagonist need to learn?

Checklist

○ Show the protagonist doesn't believe in the supernatural yet.

○ Show what internal growth the protagonist needs.

Chapter Eighteen: Resistance to the Story Goal

This scene shows the reason the protagonist doesn't want to accept the story goal in the combined skeleton blurb. In the reaction to the supernatural inciting incident, you showed the internal growth needed. You can use that in this scene to support the resistance to the story goal.

You can show this in one scene that has both the resistance to the external and the supernatural goals, or the events can occur in separate scenes.

In a fantasy, the protagonist could be scared, feel they don't have the skills, or think they aren't worthy. The main event in this scene shows the protagonist what resisting the goal means to their ordinary life.

The protagonist learns something that helps them in plot point 1.

Example Novels: Resistance to the Story Goal

Fourth Wing by Rebecca Yarros

As the names of the dead cadets are read, Violet realizes that everyone around her knows they could die at any time. Violet still hasn't accepted the goal of surviving the year, but she is acutely aware that she might not. Even though the supernatural inciting incident showed her she could control a dragon's behavior using her intelligence, she doesn't believe this yet. She must learn to trust her abilities, or she won't achieve the story goal.

This is in the same scene as the reaction to the supernatural inciting incident. Again, we note how flexible this outline is.

Twilight by Stephenie Meyer

The resistance to the external story goal is when Bella says no to the boys who want to go to the upcoming dance with her. She says she is going out of town.

The resistance to the supernatural story goal scene shows the sight of blood makes Bella nauseous. The question is, how can she accept the story goal of living with vampires if she can't tolerate the sight of blood?

The Unbroken by C. L. Clark

Touraine is harassed by friends about executing someone who knew her. She still believes life is fair as a soldier and doesn't know she needs freedom yet. She is resisting a rebellion.

A Court of Thorns and Roses by Sarah J. Maas

In the previous scene, Feyre learned Tamlin will care for her family as long as she doesn't escape. In that scene, Feyre learns Tamlin is High Fae—meaning he is a ruler in Prythian. She also learns Andras was the wolf she killed. This creates internal conflict.

This scene introduces a helper character. Alis works as a maid. Feyre's goal is to win over Alis so Alis can help her escape. Alis helps Feyre dress and gives her advice on how to be safe. Feyre chooses pants instead of a dress because it will make escaping easier. She doesn't know her true story goal yet and is resisting that goal by planning to escape.

Legendborn by Tracy Deonn

Bree is in the Order's mansion and fights her urge to run away. She desperately wants to return to her ordinary world that doesn't include oaths. She resists this urge because she knows if she runs, she will never find out who killed her mother. This is the information the reader needs in order to believe Bree will willingly take the oath in the external plot point 1 main event. Bree also learns that if she lies while taking the oath, she will die. This sets up the external plot point 1 to be full of tension.

This is the same scene as the lead-up to the external plot point 1.

A Game of Thrones by George R. R. Martin

Daenerys is promised in marriage by her brother to Khal Drogo. She doesn't want to marry him. This is the resistance to the supernatural story goal because if she doesn't marry him, she won't become the mother of dragons and the Dothraki leader.

Resistance to the Story Goal Patterns

All the scenes show the protagonist is not ready to accept the story goal. They lack skills or knowledge. Four of the books have both the external and the supernatural resistance to the story goal in the same scene. In *Twilight* and in *A Game of Thrones*, these are in separate scenes.

>Violet has no skills as a warrior.

>Bella can't tolerate the sight of blood.

>Touraine thinks she can remain a good soldier.

Feyre still plans to escape Prythian.

Bree thinks it's too dangerous to find out who killed her mother.

Daenerys resists the supernatural story goal by not wanting to marry Drogo. Eddard turns away from the North and doesn't understand his role in protecting all humans.

Your Fun Task

Actions

For Outlining:

Create the main event for the resistance to the story goal and add it to your fantasy vault.

For Editing:

In one to two sentences, summarize the main event for resistance to the story goal and add it to your fantasy vault.

Decision

While outlining, make the following decision and add it to your fantasy vault:

- Will the resistance to both the external and the supernatural story goals be in the same or separate scenes?

Checklist

- Show why the protagonist doesn't want to accept the story goal in the combined skeleton blurb.

- Show the protagonist is missing skills or knowledge.

Chapter Nineteen: Lead-Up to the External Plot Point 1

The purpose of this scene is to show that a real or metaphorical death is the possible consequence of the main event in the upcoming plot point 1 scene.

The main event must make the acceptance of the external goal in plot point 1 believable.

The protagonist still hasn't accepted the external story goal, and this scene is their last chance to walk away from the adventure. The stakes in this scene are high enough that a reader believes the protagonist's motivation for accepting the story goal.

The placement and length of this event are variable. Take note of this as you read through the example novels.

Example Novels: Lead-Up to the External Plot Point 1

Fourth Wing by Rebecca Yarros

Violet goes into the forest at night and collects plants that she can turn into poison. She's using her intelligence to achieve the external story goal. In the upcoming external plot point 1, Violet will beat an opponent on the mat by using poison to weaken but not kill them. She must become strong enough to kill another person. This shows Violet needs to grow internally if she wants to live.

She discovers Xaden plotting with others. She faces him alone, and he lets her live. Note that she faces death in this scene and in the external plot point 1.

The lead-up to external plot point 1 occurs several scenes before plot point 1. This illustrates that the exact placement is not important. It's that the lead-up comes before plot point 1 to make sure plot point 1 is believable.

Twilight by Stephenie Meyer

Bella's dad tells her that he told her mom about the accident. She is furious with him and knows she'll have to talk with her mom. This anger makes the external plot point 1 believable because she knows her mom will want her to do something she doesn't want to do—leave Forks and return to her mother. She'll use her anger to be strong in the upcoming event.

This is a hint that she will face a metaphorical death in plot point 1 where her mother begs her to return home and leave Edward.

This event occurs in the same scene and just paragraphs before the external plot point 1. The event is shown in a few paragraphs. The external plot is less important than the supernatural, so the author made the good decision to give this event less page time.

The Unbroken by C. L. Clark

Touraine has been arrested for murder and stands to be executed. Princess Luca will decide her fate. This opens the possibility that Touraine lives or dies in the next scene. Captain Rogan has also threatened that during the time between the guilty verdict and the administration of the death penalty, he will assault her. It makes the external plot point 1 believable because Touraine chooses life with Princess Luca instead of death.

A Court of Thorns and Roses by Sarah J. Maas

Feyre and Tamlin talk about the knife she stole to protect herself, and Tamlin gives genuine advice on how to best a fae and to use her skills at eavesdropping to learn something valuable. This is used later in the story when Feyre uses information she overhears to know that Tamlin has a stone heart.

He tells her there is a force plaguing the lands. She's worried she won't survive if she's caught up in it. This shows her motivation to figure out the curse. By choosing to figure out the curse, she will save her own life.

Legendborn by Tracy Deonn

The supernatural plot point 1 occurs before this scene. Bree fought supernatural Hellhounds and won. She has already accepted the supernatural story goal.

This event occurs in the same scene as the resistance to the story goal. Bree fights her urge to run away from the Order. She desperately wants to return to her ordinary world that doesn't include oaths. She resists this urge because she knows if she runs, she will never find out who killed her mother. This is the information the reader needs to believe Bree will willingly take the oath in the external plot point 1. Bree also learns that if she lies while taking the oath, she will die. This sets up the external plot point 1 to be full of tension.

A Game of Thrones by George R. R. Martin

Catelyn Stark learns the dagger used to stab her son belonged to Tyrion Lannister. She swears someone will die for this. This opens the possibility that a character belonging to the group protagonist lives or dies in the next scene.

We learn from this example that scenes in a novel written with a group protagonist can be written from any of the characters' points of view.

Lead-Up to External the Plot Point 1 Patterns

The scenes show a real or metaphorical death is the possible consequence of the main event in plot point 1.

> Violet is preparing for a battle where she could die.
>
> Bella will face a metaphorical death in plot point 1 where her mother begs her to return home and leave Edward.
>
> Touraine has been arrested for murder and stands to be executed.
>
> Feyre understands the forces that plague the fae lands will kill her.
>
> Bree learns that if she lies while taking the oath, she will die.
>
> Catelyn swears someone will die because they stabbed her son Bran.

The placement of this event varies from novel to novel. Where you place this scene is up to you.

In *Fourth Wing*, the event occurs several scenes before the external plot point 1. The event is shown in a full scene.

In *Twilight* the event occurs in the same scene and just paragraphs before the external plot point 1. The event is shown in a few paragraphs.

In *The Unbroken* and *Legendborn,* this event is the scene right before the external plot point 1.

In *A Court of Thorns and Roses*, this event occurs two scenes before the external plot point 1.

In *A Game of Thrones*, this event is shown as a full scene.

Your Fun Task

Actions

For Outlining:

Create the main event for the lead-up to the external plot point 1 and add it to your fantasy vault.

For Editing:

In one to two sentences, summarize the main event for the lead-up to the external plot point 1 and add it to your fantasy vault.

Decision

While outlining, make the following decisions and add them to your fantasy vault:

- Will the scene show a real or metaphorical death is the possible consequence?

- Will the scene stand on its own or be part of another scene?

- Where will the scene be places relative to the external plot point 1.

Checklist

○ Foreshadow a real or metaphorical death coming in plot point 1.

Chapter Twenty: External Plot Point 1 Adventure Accepted

If the protagonist doesn't accept the adventure, the story does not meet the genre requirements.

Plot point 1 is the point of no return for the protagonist. This is where they accept the story goal.

Plot point 1 must do the following:

1. Contain new information about the story goal.

2. Change the story direction.

3. Raise the stakes.

4. Be full of tension.

5. Be written in the protagonist's POV.

Fantasy Genre-Specific Duties

The main event shows the protagonist accepting the adventure and why they can't change this decision. If they can change the decision, the story is not moving forward.

By this point, the protagonist is still figuring out who they are in the context of the adventure, but they don't have all the information to truly know. From here until the middle plot point, they are going to react to events. Keep in mind, they won't be passive as they react.

The protagonist reacts to events until the middle plot point in an active manner.

Example Novels External Plot Point 1

To make it easy for you to relate the events in each of these scenes to the main story goal, we've included the skeleton blurb for each book.

Fourth Wing by Rebecca Yarros

External Plot: Violet must use her intelligence to fight other students in the Riders Quadrant; otherwise, she won't survive her first year as a cadet.

Violet beats an opponent on the mat by using poison to weaken but not kill them. She has chosen to use her intelligence to survive her first year as a cadet, thus accepting the external story goal. Violet still doesn't believe she can live up to her mother's expectations of surviving, but she's going to try.

Twilight by Stephenie Meyer

External Plot: Bella must learn to live with her father in a new town; otherwise, her mother will not have a new life.

After the accident, Bella's mother begs her to come home, but she stays in Forks because she is consumed with Edward. She has accepted the goal of making a new life in Forks. This occurs early in the novel, but it works because the supernatural plot is more important and the supernatural plot point 1 occurs right when it should.

The Unbroken by C. L. Clark

External Plot: Touraine must choose the winning side in the battle between the empire, her homeland, and the Shālan; otherwise, she will die.

Princess Luca offers Touraine a job as her assistant as an alternative to being executed. Touraine accepts and cannot go back to life as a cadet. Her definition of who she is has changed. She must move forward into Princess Luca's world. Touraine doesn't know yet that she will be the key to helping the rebellion, which includes her mother, succeed.

A Court of Thorns and Roses by Sarah J. Maas

External Plot: Feyre must find a way to leave Prythian; otherwise, she will never see her family again.

Feyre steals a knife. She decides to keep the promise she made to her mother to take care of her sisters. She accepts the story goal of returning home. She doesn't know yet this is the wrong story goal.

Legendborn by Tracy Deonn

External Plot: Bree must search for the truth about her mother's death; otherwise, she won't understand her heritage and how to live among the supernatural.

Bree takes the oath, so she can stay inside of the group and find out who killed her mother.

A Game of Thrones by George R. R. Martin

External Plot: The humans must choose the best leader to sit on the Iron Throne; otherwise; the kingdoms will fall apart.

Eddard and Catelyn make a plan to protect the North if war breaks out. Eddard is going to stay in King's Landing to protect the king. Without the right king, the kingdoms will fall apart. Eddard has accepted the goal of choosing the right leader to sit on the throne.

The reaction to plot point 1 shows this king is bankrupting the land, so Eddard has chosen the wrong story goal.

Plot Point 1 Patterns

The protagonists from all six novels accept the external story goal. They need to accept the adventure to achieve the supernatural story goal. This doesn't mean the external plot point 1 must come before the supernatural plot point 1. The placement of the scenes is up to you.

Check that the protagonist can't change this decision. If they can, the event still needs to be stronger. In the six novels:

> Violet can't change her decision to stay alive using her intelligence because she will die.

> Bella can't change her decision to live in Forks because she will ruin her mother's new life.

> Touraine can't change her decision to work with Princess Luca because she will die.

> Feyre can't change her decision to return home because she will never see her family again.

Bree can't undo the oath, because she will be killed.

Eddard must accept the goal of staying in King's Landing to protect the king, or the wrong king will come into power and weaken the kingdom. This will give the wrong family power.

Your Fun Task

Actions

For Outlining:

Create the main event for the external plot point 1 and add it to your fantasy vault.

For Editing:

In one to two sentences, summarize the main event for the external plot point 1 and add it to your fantasy vault.

Decision

While outlining, make the following decision and add it to your fantasy vault:

- Does this scene come before or after the supernatural plot point 1?

Checklist

○ Show the protagonist accepting the adventure.

- Contain new information about the story goal.

- Change the story direction.

- Raise the stakes.

- Is full of tension.

- Is written in the protagonist's POV.

- Protagonist can't change the decision to accept the story goal.

Chapter Twenty-One: Reaction to the External Plot Point 1

In a scene previous to the reaction to the external plot point 1, the protagonist accepted the external story goal. In a fantasy, this means the protagonist accepted the adventure.

The purpose of this scene is to show how the main event in the external plot point 1 impacts the protagonist. This means showing a character trait that will help or hinder the protagonist in achieving their external story goal.

You can use this scene to show character growth when you compare the trait shown here to the trait shown in the reaction to the external inciting incident.

Example Novels: Reaction to External Plot Point 1

Fourth Wing by Rebecca Yarros

Xaden shows Violet how to win without poisoning her opponents by demonstrating how to give a lethal blow using a dagger. Violet's confidence grows, but she's also confused about why Xaden is helping her.

This reminds the reader about the ordinary world Violet came from. In chapter one, Violet's sister repacks Violet's bag and gives her better boots so she will survive crossing the parapet. This scene reinforces that Violet needs help from others and she's starting to accept that.

Twilight by Stephenie Meyer

Bella goes on a girls' shopping trip. By not going alone, she is socializing with her peers and creating friendships that will keep her in Forks. This is her reaction to not wanting to leave.

She asks her friend if it's normal for the Cullens to go away and learns they only leave when the weather is sunny. She's testing her knowledge that Edward is a vampire.

She leaves her friends to find a bookshop that might have more information about vampires and ends up alone in an alley. Edward saves her from a gang of attackers, reinforcing the inciting incident where she decides what's best for herself without consulting others. This trait will get her into trouble again. The event foreshadows the climax because in the climax she leaves her friends, and Edward has to save her.

Edward tells Bella about his mind reading ability and how he found her.

Her reaction to believing Edward is a vampire is to get him to trust her and admit what he is. Even though the scene is the reaction to the external plot point 1, it is intertwined with the supernatural plot.

The Unbroken by C. L. Clark

Touraine arrives at Princess Luca's home and is surprised Luca is not surrounded by opulence. Instead, she lives in a room full of books. Touraine compares how much room Princess Luca has to the size of her barracks. Touraine is self-conscious in her rough clothing and understands she doesn't fit into this new world. Her external story goal is to choose the winning side in the battle between the empire, her homeland, and the Shālan. This scene explores Touraine in a new place in society where she doesn't fit in. This reinforces the opening image where she comes to a new place and feels uncomfortable.

A Court of Thorns and Roses by Sarah J. Maas

Feyre returns to hunting using the information Lucien (a fae) gives her. She chooses to trust Lucien. She questions why the land is empty, although it feels alive. She questions her shortcomings, but she also sets the snare to catch a Suriel. She needs the Suriel to tell her how to get home. This scene reinforces the opening image where Feyre is hunting and shows her need to take care of others.

Legendborn by Tracy Deonn

Bree is shocked Nick didn't tell her he is a descendant of King Arthur and is his Scion. No one notices Bree didn't take the oath. She worries she's made a mistake because she didn't think about what faking the oath meant to the others. This shows her trait of caring for people and makes future scenes believable when she puts herself in harm's way to protect or help others.

Not taking the oath sets up the supernatural climax where Bree is the one that removes Excalibur from the stone and is King Arthur's descendant.

A Game of Thrones by George R. R. Martin

In the reaction to the external plot point 1, Eddard decides to discover who murdered the Hand of the King. And while he does this, he learns the dismal state of the kingdom's finances. Eddard is shown King Robert Baratheon is bankrupting the kingdom, and he believes this is a misunderstanding. This scene shows how Eddard puts trust in others when he shouldn't and trusting others will hurt him later in the story.

Reaction to Plot Point 1 Patterns

All the scenes show how the protagonist feels and the actions they take because of the main event in the external plot point 1. The reader is shown the character trait that will help or hinder the protagonist in achieving their story goal. The reaction to the inciting incident also did this but showed a different character trait.

Here we show the character trait in the reaction to plot point 1 versus the reaction to the inciting incident for the six novels.

> In *Fourth Wing*, this scene reinforces that Violet needs help from others. In the reaction to the external inciting incident, Violet trained for six months to learn to fight, showing she is willing to try.

> In *Twilight*, this scene reinforces the inciting incident where Bella decides what's best for herself without consulting others. In the reaction to the external inciting incident, Bella is willing to adapt to a new environment.

> In *The Unbroken*, this scene reinforces the opening image where Touraine comes to a new place and feels uncomfortable. In the reaction to the external inciting incident, Touraine obeys orders at all costs.

> In *A Court of Thorns and Roses*, this scene reinforces the opening image where Feyre is hunting and shows her need to take care of others. In the reaction to the external

inciting incident, Feyre's trait is that she is willing to sacrifice herself for others.

In *Legendborn*, this scene shows her trait of caring for others and makes future scenes believable when she puts herself in harm's way to protect or help others. In the reaction to the external inciting incident, Bree is stubborn and does what she feels is right for herself.

In *A Game of Thrones*, this scene shows how Eddard puts trust in others when he shouldn't. In the reaction to the external inciting incident, Eddard is loyal to the crown over his family.

Your Fun Task

Actions

For Outlining:

Create the main event for the reaction to the external plot point 1 and add it to your fantasy vault.

For Editing:

In one to two sentences, summarize the main event for the reaction to the external plot point 1 and add it to your fantasy vault.

Decision

While outlining, make the following decision and add it to your fantasy vault:

- What character trait will help or hinder the protagonist in achieving their external story goal?

Checklist

Ensure the scene covers each item in this list.

- Show how the protagonist feels as a result of the main event in the external plot point 1 scene.

- Show a character trait that is different from the character trait shown in the reaction to the external inciting incident.

Chapter Twenty-Two: Lead-up to the Supernatural Plot Point 1

The lead-up to the supernatural plot point 1 scene has similar duties as the lead-up to the external plot point 1 scene. The protagonist hasn't accepted the supernatural story goal, and this scene is their last chance to walk away from the adventure.

This scene often shows the protagonist alone or trying to be alone.

You can also foreshadow that the protagonist's life could be at stake in the supernatural plot point 1 and make that plot point believable.

Example Novels: Lead-Up to the Supernatural Plot Point 1

Fourth Wing by Rebecca Yarros

Violet is alone when she sees Jack and others tracking a small dragon. She warns the dragon (Andarna). This opens the possibility that Violet lives or dies in the next scene (supernatural plot point 1).

Tairn, the most powerful dragon, understands Violet will give up her life for Andarna.

There is a supernatural element in when Tairn speaks to Violet telepathically.

When Violet says the name of two dragons at the threshing in the supernatural plot point 1, the reader believes it's possible because

Violet has shown she is worthy of the dragons by protecting Andarna.

Twilight by Stephenie Meyer

When Bella is on her shopping trip, she wanders off on her own and ends up alone on an isolated street. A gang approaches and threatens her. She prepares to fight them, and her life is at stake. This sets up the situation where Edward must help her.

The Unbroken by C. L. Clark

Touraine is alone in jail and has been charged with treason. She's treated poorly. Captain Rogan comes to get her and drags her to the court. Touraine is told the trial will not go well for her. This sets up the tension and stakes for the supernatural plot point 1.

A Court of Thorns and Roses by Sarah J. Maas

Feyre is trying to be alone with Lucien because she wants to persuade him to speak to Tamlin on her behalf. Before she can get to Lucien, Tamlin finds her in the garden and offers to spend the day with her, showing her the grounds. She rejects him. Her goal is to get Lucien to help her return home. She doesn't understand yet the danger the supernatural poses to her.

Legendborn by Tracy Deonn

Bree wants to be alone in this scene and when she meets Nick, she tries to get away from him. This leads perfectly into the supernatural plot point 1. Her life will be in danger from the magic she sees.

A Game of Thrones by George R. R. Martin

Daenerys is alone riding when Ser Jorah slows his horse beside her. Daenerys rides with Ser Jorah and they talk about the lands. Then she commands everyone to leave her while she rides off. She needs to be alone again.

Lead-Up to the Supernatural Plot Point 1 Patterns

Each of the protagonists is alone at some point in the scene or wants to be alone.

> Violet is alone when she sees Jack and others tracking a small dragon.
>
> When Bella is on her shopping trip, she wanders off and ends up alone on an isolated street.
>
> Touraine is alone in jail and has been charged with treason.
>
> Feyre is trying to be alone with Lucien because she wants to persuade him to speak to Tamlin on her behalf.
>
> Bree wants to be alone and when she meets Nick, she tries to get away from him.
>
> Daenerys is alone riding when Ser Jorah slows his horse beside her. Daenerys rides with Ser Jorah and they talk about the lands. Then she commands everyone to leave her while she rides off. She needs to be alone again.

Your Fun Task

Actions

For Outlining:

Create the main event for the lead-up to the supernatural plot point 1 and add it to your fantasy vault.

For Editing:

In one to two sentences, summarize the main event for the lead-up to the supernatural plot point 1 and add it to your fantasy vault.

Decision

While outlining, make the following decision and add it to your fantasy vault:

- How will time alone put the protagonist in peril?

Checklist

○ Foreshadow the protagonist's life could be at stake in the supernatural plot point 1.

○ Make the supernatural plot point 1 be believable.

○ Show the protagonist alone or their desire to be alone.

Chapter Twenty-Three: Supernatural Plot Point 1

The protagonist fully believes in the supernatural, or they use it for the first time.

The main event foreshadows how the protagonist will address the supernatural climax.

The protagonist must accept both the supernatural and external story goals, or the story is not a fantasy.

Example Novels Supernatural Plot Point 1

Fourth Wing by Rebecca Yarros

Violet bonds with Tairn and Andarna at the Threshing ceremony. She is the first cadet to bond with two dragons. This allows her to accept the story goal of using her signet because she has bonded with two dragons and Tairn is the most powerful dragon. Bonding is for life, so Violet cannot turn back.

Up to this point, Violet did not believe she could live up to her mother's expectations that she could survive her first year as a cadet. Here she believes it might be possible. She needed both the external and supernatural plot point 1 events to give her a bit of confidence.

This shows us how external and supernatural events can be woven together.

Violet fully believes in the supernatural because she has bonded with two dragons. This foreshadows both dragons helping Violet in the climax.

In the supernatural climax, Violet needs both bonded dragons to succeed.

Twilight by Stephenie Meyer

Bella learns about Edward's magic after he protects her from a gang of attackers and admits he found her by following her scent and knew she was in trouble by reading the others' minds. Edward admits to Bella he is a vampire.

This is the supernatural plot point 1 because she has proof Edward is a vampire and is her first step in learning to live with vampires.

In this scene and the climax scene, Bella goes alone to dangerous places and Edward saves her. This scene foreshadows the supernatural climax where Edward saves Bella from her vampire attacker.

The Unbroken by C. L. Clark

At her court martial, Touraine mentions Shālan magic. She shares that the Brigāni might use magic against the Balladaire. The accusers don't believe her, but the information drives Princess Luca to save her. Touraine has started the search for the healing magic. She has to find the source of the magic if she is to save her people.

These events show how Touraine uses magic to save herself in this scene and foreshadows how she will use magic in the supernatural climax to save herself again.

A Court of Thorns and Roses by Sarah J. Maas

Feyre comes in contact with a Bogge. The Bogge speaks to Feyre telepathically. If she looks at it, it will kill her. She is successful in not looking at the creature and understands that the supernatural is dangerous in Prythian. Lucien has shown her she must depend on other fairies if she is going to survive in this world. She accepts the goal of breaking an ancient curse.

Lucien had previously caused her harm, but here, he helps her. This foreshadows the climax where she must trust a fairy who caused her harm before and is trying to help her.

Legendborn by Tracy Deonn

Bree met Nick for the first time in the previous scene when supernatural hounds attacked them. Bree stays and fights the Hellhounds, and they almost kill her, but Nick saves her from death.

This is the start of her supernatural journey.

The main event in this part of the scene foreshadows the climax where Bree uses Excalibur to kill supernatural creatures. Again, another male helps her not die. In the supernatural climax, King Arthur channels his ability to fight through her to save everyone. And here, in this scene, Nick saves her. And at the end of both scenes she collapses.

A Game of Thrones by George R. R. Martin

Daenerys dreams of dragons and feels warmth in their eggs. She decides to become Khaleesi instead of killing herself. She has accepted the supernatural goal.

This foreshadows the main event in the supernatural climax where Daenerys takes her dragon eggs into the fire and comes out the literal mother of dragons.

Supernatural Plot Point 1 Patterns

Something supernaturally significant occurs for each of the protagonists.

Violet bonds with dragons.

Bella gets Edward to admit he is a vampire.

Touraine makes it public to her enemies that healing magic might exist.

Feyre learns she can protect herself from the supernatural.

Bree fights the supernatural hounds.

Daenerys chooses to become the Khaleesi.

We can see each protagonist has accepted the supernatural story goal. This is half of the combined story goal.

The main event in the supernatural plot point 1 foreshadows the main event in the supernatural climax.

> In this scene, Violet bonds with two dragons. In the supernatural climax scene in *Fourth Wing*, Violet needs both bonded dragons to succeed.

In this scene in *Twilight*, Bella goes along to dangerous places and Edward saves her. This scene foreshadows the supernatural climax where Edward saves Bella from her vampire attacker.

The events in this scene in *The Unbroken* show how Touraine uses magic to save herself and foreshadows how she will use magic in the supernatural climax to save herself again.

In *A Court of Thorns and Roses*, Lucien had previously caused Feyre harm, but in this scene he helps her. This foreshadows the climax where she must trust a fairy who caused her harm before and is trying to help her.

In *Legendborn*, this scene foreshadows the climax scene where Bree uses Excalibur to kill supernatural creatures. In the supernatural climax scene, King Arthur channels his ability to fight through her to save everyone. In both scenes, another character helps her stay alive.

In *A Game of Thrones*, Daenerys dreams of dragons and feels warmth in their eggs. She decides to become Khaleesi instead of killing herself. This foreshadows the supernatural climax where Daenerys takes her dragon eggs into the fire and comes out the literal mother of dragons.

Your Fun Task

Actions

For Outlining:

Create the main event for the supernatural plot point 1 and add it to your fantasy vault.

For Editing:

In one to two sentences, summarize the main event for the supernatural plot point 1 and add it to your fantasy vault.

Decision

While outlining, make the following decision and add it to your fantasy vault:

- What supernaturally significant event occurs for the protagonist?

Checklist

○ The supernatural is part of this scene.

○ Show the protagonist accepting the supernatural goal.

○ Foreshadow an event in the supernatural climax.

Chapter Twenty-Four: Reaction to the Supernatural Plot Point 1

In a scene previous to the reaction to the supernatural plot point 1, the protagonist accepted the supernatural story goal. In a fantasy, this means the protagonist has accepted the supernatural is part of their life.

This scene shows how the protagonist is stronger because of the main event in the supernatural plot point 1. The protagonist learns what they have to lose if they can't control the supernatural.

By the end of the story, the protagonists must use the supernatural to achieve the supernatural climax.

Example Novels: Reaction to the Supernatural Plot Point 1

Fourth Wing by Rebecca Yarros

The generals resist allowing Violet to bond with two dragons. Violet refuses to have her wound treated by the healer because she understands she can't appear weak.

Later in the novel, the unbonded riders try to kill Violet because they want to bond with Tairn, the strongest dragon, so this sets up difficulties for Violet.

Violet also has time to process her feelings toward Jack. She is no longer scared of him, as he was the one to run away from the dragons in the lead-up to the supernatural plot point 1. She recognizes she is braver than Jack.

Later in the same scene, Violet learns that her dragon and Xaden's are a mated pair. If Violet dies, Xaden dies too. Two dragons and two people are linked forever. They cannot return to being individuals.

Twilight by Stephenie Meyer

Edward drops Bella at home. She knows Edward is a vampire and is dangerous. Her emotional reaction to the knowledge is that she loves him. The knowledge that Edward is dangerous, and the fact that she is in love with him sets up the stakes. Bella is in a stronger place because Edward trusts her and will protect her.

The Unbroken by C. L. Clark

As soon as Touraine mentions healing magic, she notices Princess Luca is keenly interested in her. She uses this to her advantage and asks Princess Luca to spare her life. She's bold and tells Luca that she saved her life and Luca owes her. Touraine directs her emotional stress at others at the court martial and not at Luca. This is a key moment for Touraine, showing her strength. Touraine knows death awaits her if she fails.

A Court of Thorns and Roses by Sarah J. Maas

Feyre uses the event in plot point 1 to remind herself the fairy world is dangerous and uses the interaction with the Bogge to justify killing the wolf.

She takes an hour to calm down and speak with Lucien about what happened in the supernatural plot point 1. She worries Lucien would be capable of killing her. By the end of the scene, she's made a tentative truce with Lucien even though he could be dangerous.

Legendborn by Tracy Deonn

Bree finds herself in the hands of a healer, William, who is fixing her wounds. She is shocked by the things she learns. Even though Nick saved her, she's afraid of him. To protect herself, she hides information from Nick. This shows she's concerned with self-preservation. She understands that death is a possibility if she is too open. This will protect her later in the story.

A Game of Thrones by George R. R. Martin

The Dothraki choose Daenerys over her brother, giving her the power of a Khaleesi. This is a short paragraph and shows the power of hitting the beats but not needing to have a full scene.

Reaction to Supernatural Plot Point 1 Patterns

The protagonists are all stronger because of the supernatural plot point 1.

In *Fourth Wing*, Violet is bonded with two dragons.

In *Twilight*, Bella is in a stronger place because Edward trusts her and will protect her.

In *The Unbroken*, Touraine gets Princess Luca on her side because of her knowledge of magic. She needs Luca if she is going to survive.

In *A Court of Thorns and Roses*, Feyre makes a tentative truce with Lucien. She needs him if she is going to survive.

In *Legendborn*, Bree understands that death is a possibility if she is too open with others. The knowledge makes her stronger.

In *A Game of Thrones*, the Dothraki choose Daenerys over her brother, giving her the power of a Khaleesi. The position makes her stronger.

Your Fun Task

Actions

For Outlining:

Create the main event for the reaction to the supernatural plot point 1 and add it to your fantasy vault.

For Editing:

In one to two sentences, summarize the main event for the reaction to the supernatural plot point 1 and add it to your fantasy vault.

Decision

While outlining, make the following decision and add it to your fantasy vault:

- How will the protagonist be stronger?

Checklist

- Show the protagonist getting stronger.
- The story stakes are clear.

Chapter Twenty-Five: Goal Attempts

To move the story forward after plot point 1, the protagonist must try to achieve the story goal. For a goal to create tension for the length of the story, the protagonist cannot achieve the goal easily; otherwise, the story would be over.

The focus on not fully achieving the goal is important, so plot point 1 to the middle plot point is about the protagonist attempting to achieve the story goal and then learning from what they have attempted.

Whether they are successful or not is dictated by the plot.

There are a minimum three types of goal attempts. The attempts can be in any order, and they can succeed or fail. We've listed these here to spark your imagination. The protagonist's goal attempts can be related to learning from:

- trusting another
- history
- their actions

You'll create a main event for each of the goal attempts and decide if the protagonist is successful or not. They may fail but come away with precious insights.

These scenes provide a good opportunity for the protagonist to make a choice. Either they learn a lesson or not.

If all attempts succeed, the reader won't worry about the protagonist achieving their story goal, and the story lacks tension. If all attempts fail, the story will feel monotonous and the reader may lose interest.

There is an exception here. If the protagonist dies by the end of the story, failing all goal attempts can foreshadow the death.

You defined two story goals. One for the external plot and one for the supernatural plot. Try to have three goal attempts for each story goal. This gives you a ton of flexibility for writing your unique story. There should be at least one strong goal attempt for each of the external and the supernatural goals.

One main event can show a goal attempt for both the external and supernatural story goals.

The goal attempts can start after the first plot point 1 occurs. When the external plot point occurs before the supernatural plot point 1, the first external goal attempt can be placed between these scenes. It cannot be placed before both plot point 1 scenes because the protagonist has not accepted either story goal yet.

All three goals shouldn't come between the two plot point 1 scenes because one goal has not been accepted yet by the protagonist and the reader will expect to see the protagonist attempting both goals.

All goals can come after both plot point 1 scenes, and all need to be included before the first middle plot point.

Example Novels: Goal Attempts

For the goal attempts in each novel, we are not showing all attempts. We are illustrating options for this section of your novel.

Fourth Wing by Rebecca Yarros

External Goal Attempts

Violet recites the codex to prevent disqualification from an obstacle course, which shows her knowledge from being a scribe will help her survive. The external goal attempt is successful and foreshadows learning from history will save her life. This goal attempt shows learning from history.

The scene is placed after the external plot point 1 but before the supernatural plot point 1.

Xaden's cohort protects Violet. Imogen is part of that cohort and wants to train Violet. Tairn tells Violet she can trust Imogen. Violet trusts Tairn, so she trains with Imogen. This is her second goal attempt to survive the year, and she succeeds. This goal attempt shows learning through trusting another.

Violet stands up to Dain and tells him there is never going to be anything between them because he has no faith in her. By actively confronting Dain about his lack of belief in her, she is learning to follow through with her gut instincts. She needs to know who to trust and who not to trust, so this learning helps her ability to survive. The next beat, where she flips her finger at Xaden, shows that she has not fully understood how to act. This goal attempt shows learning through action.

Note that all three goal attempts occur after the external plot point 1.

Supernatural Goal Attempts

Tairn and Violet train together, but she can't stay seated on his back. She must learn to stay seated or she won't survive the year. After feeling stronger in the reaction to the supernatural plot point 1, Violet now feels weak again. She can't see how she will survive if she can't stay on Tairn's back. This is an unsuccessful goal attempt and shows Violet trying to learn from action.

Violet looks for books on venin and wyvern magic. Other riders get their signet, while Violet doesn't. She can't fully bond to Tairn without a signet, and she will die. This is a failed goal attempt because she doesn't learn enough about venin and wyvern. This scene shows Violet trying to gain the knowledge she needs to address the story goal and is learning through history.

When an intrinsic's signet manifests, showing he can read everyone's thoughts, Violet is worried the new dragon rider will read her mind. She trusts Xaden's advice to think of other things. She learns to trust Xaden when he advises her on how to control herself when others try to use their magic on her. This is a successful goal attempt showing Violet learning to trust.

Twilight by Stephenie Meyer

External Goal Attempt

Jacob's father and Bella's father fall out over the Cullens (Edward's family). There is a history where the werewolves and the humans in Forks are at odds over how to treat the Cullens. Bella's father defends the Cullens. Bella does not ask for more information, and so she fails to learn from history. This is a failed goal attempt.

Edward and Bella pretend to be dating. The day after the reaction to the supernatural plot point 1, Edward drives Bella to school. They run into her friend and Edward reads her mind. The friend wants to know if Bella and Edward are dating and how Bella feels about Edward. The goal of the fake dating is to make life at school easier and to stop people from asking questions about Bella and Edward. They agree to tell others they are dating, and Bella is hurt by

Edward's lack of enthusiasm. This combined supernatural and external goal attempt shows learning through action.

This is the first attempt to live in Forks with vampires and near Edward. It succeeds at making life easier but fails at giving Bella confidence in her relationship with Edward. The external goal attempt is successful, and the supernatural goal attempt fails.

Edward tries to protect Bella by desensitizing himself to her. He tells Bella he cares as much about her as she does about him. They plan an outing alone. Edward admits to killing bears for their blood instead of people. Edward touches Bella for the first time. This is a major step forward in their relationship. As part of learning to live with vampires, Bella wants to include Edward in her life and brings him home. Jacob and his dad find Bella and Edward in the driveway. The goal attempt fails because Bella is now in conflict with the werewolves and can't give her father time to get to know Edward. This combined supernatural and external goal attempt shows learning to trust another.

This scene shows Bella learning to trust in the context of the supernatural story goal but failing to trust her father with Edward's true nature. This is a failed goal attempt because this pushes her away from her external goal to live in Forks.

The external and supernatural goal attempts occur after both plot point 1 scenes.

The Unbroken by C. L. Clark

External Goal Attempts

Touraine goes to a funeral for her soldiers. She tries to convince the other soldiers that she is not Princess Luca's concubine and that Luca has promised to make things better for the Sands. She attempts to convince them the Balladairans can help them. None of the soldiers believe her and they openly show their disgust at her actions. After feeling stronger in the reaction to the supernatural plot point 1 scene, Touraine's confidence is diminished. The goal attempt fails because she's still trying to be part of the conscripts, and that's the wrong goal. This goal attempt is categorized as learning through action.

Touraine tries to assimilate into Princess Luca's court. She fails at this as she is unable to control her reactions to Captain Rogan. This embarrasses Luca. This is good for her story goal, so the goal attempt is a successful because Touraine understands that Luca's world is not her own, and she cannot trust herself to be diplomatic. This goal attempt is categorized as learning through trust.

Touraine learns how to read Shālan. This scene shows Touraine trying to gain an understanding of the written words, so she can use this to further her understanding of her heritage. This goal attempt shows learning through history.

Touraine and Princess Luca are searching for a book about magic when they are attacked. Luca's guard is pushed into the water and a crocodile takes her leg. The goal attempt fails because they don't find the book. Without the book, Touraine and Luca must trade with the rebels. This goal attempt shows learning through action.

All goal attempts occur after both plot point 1 scenes.

A Court of Thorns and Roses by Sarah J. Maas

Tamlin appears in beast form. He's killed the Bogge and is hurt. Feyre treats his wounds, and they find common ground in caring for others. By helping Tamlin, she is strengthening him so that when the time comes, he can help fight the wicked curse. Feyre feels sorry for him. This is her first attempt at fitting in at Prythian and thinking of Tamlin as more than a beast.

This is an unsuccessful goal attempt because, at the end of the scene, she closes herself off to him. This hinders her from being accepted by the fairies, and that hinders her from breaking the ancient curse that is destroying Tamlin's world. After feeling strong enough in the reaction to the supernatural plot point 1 scene to make a truce with Lucien, she takes a step back from Tamlin.

The goal attempt fails because Feyre did not learn to trust Tamlin.

Feyre goes to Fire Night and almost gets killed. Rhys (a High Fae) saves her from three fairies. This action shows how dangerous the fairy world is and how they don't accept her. This is a failed supernatural goal attempt and Feyre does not learn through action.

Feyre convinces Lucien to tell her how to trap a Suriel. She believes a Suriel might have knowledge to find a loophole in the treaty, so she can go home. This resistance to the story goal leads her to learn two things. Tamlin is the high lord of the summer courts and she should stay with him; otherwise, she and her family will be killed. This is leading her to her external story goal. This goal attempt shows learning through action.

Legendborn by Tracy Deonn

In the lead-up to this scene, Sel tries to mesmerize Bree. Bree uses self-inflicted pain to avoid being mesmerized. In this scene, Bree finds Nick in class and tells him Sel failed, and she wants answers from him about the Order, the Legendborn, the Onceborn, and other mythical people. He refuses to tell her anything. He says he will no longer be her tutor and will stay away from her. This is her first attempt to get closer to the Order, and it fails. Bree shows how stubborn she is by refusing to accept this and is going to find another way. Her supernatural goal is combining root magic with Legendborn magic. In this goal attempt, even though Bree failed at achieving her goal, she's determined to find a way. This goal attempt shows learning through action.

The scene occurs after the supernatural plot point 1 and before the external plot point 1, so having a goal attempt where she is trying to achieve the supernatural goal works.

Bree accepts William's offer to teach her about their world. William shows her the Wall of Ages with the thirteen bloodlines of the Round Table. She learns Camlann is the battle between the Round Table and demons. This is a successful goal attempt because Bree learns the history she needs to move forward with the supernatural story goal. This goal attempt shows learning through history.

Bree chooses to meet with her mentor, Patricia, even though she thinks the meetings is another way for her father to keep tabs on her. By choosing to meet Patricia, she trusts her father to consider her best interests. This goal attempt shows learning through trust.

A Game of Thrones by George R. R. Martin

External Goal attempts

Eddard goes to the Grand Maester to investigate the Hand of the King's death. The Maester thinks the death was natural. This is a failed attempt because Eddard doesn't know yet the Hand of the King was murdered. Eddard's goal is to protect the King, and he won't know how serious the threat is without knowing the Hand was murdered. Eddard doesn't learn through action.

Eddard discovers the Hand of the King was searching for the king's bastard children. He reads *The Lineages and Histories of the Great Houses of the Seven Kingdoms, With Descriptions of Many High Lords and Noble Ladies and Their Children,* by Grand Maester Malleon. This is a failed attempt because he doesn't understand why the Hand of the King was interested in the children. He didn't figure out someone was killing the king's bastards. Eddard does not learn through history.

Eddard asks Varys how the Hand of the King died. Varys confirms it was poison. Eddard now knows that the Hand was murdered. This is a failed attempt because Eddard trusts the wrong person and it will lead to his death.

Supernatural Goal Attempts

Daenerys learns to ride a horse. She fails to learn from the human who is tasked with teaching her. She learns from the horse. This is the first step away from trusting humans and learning through her connection with animals. This goal attempt shows learning through trust.

Daenerys commands all to stay where they are while she rides. Her brother disagrees with her, and he hits her. The Dothraki stand by her and not her brother; this is the first time she has control over her him. She is their Khaleesi, a leader. This is part of the supernatural story goal to lead the humans. This goal attempt shows learning through action.

Daenerys tries to understand if dragons are real and listens to a folktale saying they can come back to life through fire. She laughs off the information and does not believe it. So, this is a failure to learn from history.

Goal Attempt Patterns

Of all the novels, only Bree in *Legendborn* is stronger by the end of the first goal attempt. The other protagonists are all weaker. The goal attempts either makes the protagonist stronger or weaker.

All the first goal attempts fail. In *Fourth Wing, The Unbroken,* and *A Game of Thrones* the protagonists attempt to achieve the external story goal. In *Twilight, Legendborn* and *A Court of Thorns and Roses,* the protagonists attempt to achieve the supernatural story goal.

The choice is yours to make and will affect the scene placement. Attempting the external goal means this scene occurs after the external plot point 1 scene. Attempting the supernatural goal means this scene occurs after the supernatural plot point 1 scene. Attempting both means this scene occurs after both the external and supernatural plot point 1 scenes.

Your Fun Task

Actions

For Outlining:

Create the main event for six goal attempts. Three for the external plot and three for the supernatural plot. Add the events to your fantasy vault.

For Editing:

In one to two sentences, summarize the main events for the goal attempts for the external and supernatural plots and add them to your fantasy vault. If you don't have a minimum of three goal attempts, consider writing new scenes.

Decisions

While outlining, make the following decisions and add them to your fantasy vault:

- Will this scene strengthen or weaken the protagonist?

- Will the protagonist attempt to achieve the external goal, the supernatural goal, or both?

- Will the goal attempts be a sentence, paragraph, scene, or chapter in length?

Checklist

○ The goal attempts are for at least one of the story goals, or both.

○ At least one plot point 1 occurs before the first goal attempt.

Chapter Twenty-Six: Lead-Up to the External Middle Plot Point

The protagonist is about to enter a dangerous place. This is a last moment of safety before they face death or put someone they love in danger.

Example Novels: Lead-Up to the External Middle Plot Point

Fourth Wing by Rebecca Yarros

Violet tells Tairn Jack is going to kill her when they meet on the mat. She convinces Liam, another cadet, to keep Xaden busy while she fights Jack. She knows she has to beat Jack on her own or she won't survive. This is a significant lead-up to the external middle plot point because it shows Violet wants to be proactive.

Twilight by Stephenie Meyer

Edward tells Bella he must go away and hunt if she is to be safe around him. He introduces Bella to Alice (his vampire sister), which is a move toward Bella feeling safe with the other vampires. This gives her confidence to be alone with Edward. In the external middle plot point, she will put her father's life in danger so she can be alone with Edward.

The Unbroken by C. L. Clark

Princess Luca gives Touraine her freedom papers. As part of this, Luca also agrees to give one hundred weapons to the rebels. This sets up a dangerous situation for Touraine because she will be negotiating between the rebels and Balladairans.

A Court of Thorns and Roses by Sarah J. Maas

Tamlin gives Feyre roses. She pretends they mean nothing but takes care of them. This makes the middle plot point believable because it's where they change the direction of their romance and Feyre decides she wants to help him. Helping Tamlin will put her life in danger.

Legendborn by Tracy Deonn

Bree's mentor, Patricia, teaches Bree about her ancestors' history. She tells her about root magic and that every family practices in a different way. She wants to show Bree by connecting her with her deceased female relatives. Bree puts her life in danger by agreeing to meet the dead.

A Game of Thrones by George R. R. Martin

Earlier in the story, Eddard wakes up after being unconscious for six days. Jaime Lannister wounded him and then fled the city. Catelyn has taken Tyrion prisoner. The king is angry about the fighting but forgives Eddard. This makes the queen angry because Tyrion is her brother. She will not forgive Eddard. Eddard doesn't understand how dangerous she can be.

King Robert has gone hunting, and Eddard sits in his place on the throne. He is about to make decisions to the people who kneel before him and doesn't understand how dangerous this will be for him.

Lead-Up to the External Middle Plot Point Patterns

Each protagonist puts a life in danger, either their own or someone else's.

In *Fourth Wing*, Violet puts her life in danger by convincing Liam to keep Xaden busy while she fights Jack alone.

In *Twilight*, Bella puts her father's life in danger so she can be alone with Edward.

In *The Unbroken*, Touraine puts her life in danger because she will be negotiating between the rebels and Balladairans.

In *A Court of Thorns and Roses*, Feyre puts her life in danger by helping Tamlin.

In *Legendborn*, Bree puts her life in danger by agreeing to meet the dead.

In *A Game of Thrones*, Eddard is about to put his life and his families in danger by making the wrong decisions.

Your Fun Task

Actions

For Outlining:

Create the main event for the lead-up to the middle plot point and add it to your fantasy vault.

For Editing:

In one to two sentences, summarize the main event for the lead-up to the middle plot point and add it to your fantasy vault.

Decision

While outlining, make the following decision and add it to your fantasy vault:

- Will the protagonist put their own life in danger or someone else's?

Checklist

o Show the protagonist's life or someone else's life is in danger.

Chapter Twenty-Seven: External Middle Plot Point

By this point in the external story, the conflict is becoming clearer to the protagonist and to the reader. What the protagonist doesn't know yet is how they are going to achieve the story goal.

In the middle of the external story, readers expect the protagonist's behavior to go from reactionary to proactive. The middle plot point scene should have something terrible or life-changing happen to the protagonist.

The external middle plot point must:

1. Be told from the protagonist's point of view.
2. Be written in active form.
3. Show the protagonist leading the action by the end of the scene.
4. Show the protagonist proactively wanting to address the external story goal.
5. Foreshadow the climax.

Fantasy Genre-Specific Duties

This scene will show a false victory or defeat. The protagonist will gain new information that pushes them in a new direction. Think about how this event can refine the protagonist's external goal.

The protagonist will face a difficult moment, and their life may be at stake.

The story goal can also be in jeopardy.

Example Novels: External Middle Plot Point

Fourth Wing by Rebecca Yarros

Violet poisons Jack during a match and wins. This is a false victory because Jack will try to kill Violet later in the story so she should not have let him live. Violet purposefully makes sure Xaden cannot help her beat Jack. She needs to prove she can take care of herself. By the end of the novel, she learns she needs to work with others to win.

Twilight by Stephenie Meyer

Bella tells her father that she is not going to Seattle, and so her dad offers to cancel his fishing trip. But she says there is no need. Her dad comments on how easy she is to live with. Bella is becoming proactive in creating a life in Forks. This is a false victory because she will put her father's life in danger with her actions. She is not helping him by hiding the dangers that surround them.

The Unbroken by C. L. Clark

In the previous scene, Princess Luca gave Touraine her freedom papers. As part of this, Luca also gave her one hundred weapons to take to the rebels. Touraine takes Luca to the rebels, and they agree to trade the weapons for one priest.

This is a false victory because they have been betrayed. An attack is about to occur.

A Court of Thorns and Roses by Sarah J. Maas

Feyre starts to realize her external story goal of returning home is the wrong goal. She's falling for Tamlin, and this is weakening her resolve to go home.

This is a powerful scene because it contains the external and supernatural middle plot point. In the supernatural middle plot point, Tamlin shortens a table using magic, and it takes all his energy. Feyre sees for the first time how much trouble they are in. She is shown how the masks are limiting Tamlin's magic.

Legendborn by Tracy Deonn

Patricia tells Bree she doesn't know much about her mother, but Bree thinks she knows who killed her. This is a false victory because Bree is wrong.

A Game of Thrones by George R. R. Martin

Eddard proactively acts for the king in his absence instead of waiting for him to return. He sends knights to retaliate against Clegane for plundering land. He doesn't let Ser Loras go with the knights and makes an enemy. This is a false victory because Eddard has created enemies. He believes he holds power, but he doesn't.

Middle Plot Point Patterns

Fourth Wing, *Twilight*, *The Unbroken*, *Legendborn*, and *A Game of Thrones* all show a false victory. Only *A Court of Thorns and Roses* shows a false defeat.

Two of the novels contain a supernatural element: *Legendborn* and *A Court of Thorns and Roses*. The choice is yours.

Your Fun Task

Actions

For Outlining:

Create the main event for the external middle plot point and add it to your fantasy vault.

For Editing:

In one to two sentences, summarize the main event for the external middle plot point 1 and add it to your fantasy vault.

Decisions

While outlining, make the following decisions and add them to your fantasy vault:

- Will the scene contain a false victory or false defeat?
- Will the scene contain supernatural elements?

Checklist

- Be told from the protagonist's point of view.
- Be written in active form.

- Show the protagonist leading the action by the end of the scene.

- Show the protagonist proactively wanting to address the story goal.

- Foreshadow the ending.

- Show the protagonist facing a hard moment.

- Show a false victory or defeat.

- Show the protagonist starting to understand the real story goal.

Chapter Twenty-Eight: Reaction to the External Middle Plot Point

The purpose of this scene is to show what the protagonist is internally or externally afraid of.

The scene can also show the stakes have increased.

Example Novels: Reaction to the External Middle Plot Point

Fourth Wing by Rebecca Yarros

Violet learns Rhiannon, a cadet, can summon objects. The skill is used in book two of the series. Violet doesn't understand her powers are close to being active too, so she feels pressure for her signet to appear. She is afraid she won't get powers.

Liam gifts Violet a carved sculpture of Tairn, giving meaning to their friendship. This is relevant to the climax and is going to make the climax difficult for Violet.

Violet and Dain can't get back to being friends. He started as her love interest, and now they have lost each other. Dain touches Violet's face. This is relevant later in the novel and leads to Violet and Dain becoming enemies.

The events with Liam and Dain show what Violet has to lose if she fails to achieve her external story goal.

At the end of the scene Rhiannon says Violet is the strongest rider of their generation. Violet doesn't believe this yet.

Twilight by Stephenie Meyer

Now that Bella has lied to her dad about where she will be, she reacts with fear and anticipation. She is still afraid of becoming a vampire but is determined to spend time alone with Edward to convince him to turn her into one.

She is not secure enough to tell Edward about how she feels about him. At the end of the scene, she says she never met anyone in Phoenix she ever wanted.

The Unbroken by C. L. Clark

Touraine, Princess Luca, and the rebels are attacked. The rebels instantly blame Luca. Touraine protects Luca so she can escape. She tries to convince the rebels the attack wasn't Luca's fault. Touraine is afraid that her Sands will kill her, the rebels and Luca.

A Court of Thorns and Roses by Sarah J. Maas

Feyre and Tamlin spend the day in the glen getting to know each other. Tamlin removes his glamor and shows Feyre what he looks like. She is afraid he will never be able to take off his mask so she can see all of him. She is also afraid Tamlin won't let her help him with the conflict.

Legendborn by Tracy Deonn

Bree tells William, the healer, that Sel is a Bloodcrafter and dangerous. Bloodcrafters let Hellhounds into the world twenty-five years ago. She thinks Sel is a Crossroads man and is afraid of him.

Bree is also afraid of who she is. Is she a troublemaker, or is she something better?

A Game of Thrones by George R. R. Martin

Eddard tells his daughters he's sending them north and that Sansa will not marry Joffrey. His reaction to sending knights north is to protect his daughters from an upcoming war. He is afraid for them and believes they will be safer in Winterfell.

Reaction to the External Middle Plot Point Patterns

Each protagonist is afraid of something external or internal. In four of the books, *Fourth Wing, The Unbroken, Legendborn, A Game of Thrones,* the protagonist is afraid for themselves. In *Twilight*, and *A Court of Thorns and Roses* the protagonists are afraid for their love interest and are feeling they are not enough.

In *Fourth Wing*, Violet is afraid her powers won't appear. She is also afraid of who she is.

In *Twilight*, Bella is still afraid of becoming a vampire. She is also afraid to admit to Edward her feelings for him.

In *The Unbroken*, Touraine is afraid Luca will die and afraid her betrayal will mean her Sands will kill her. She is afraid of who she is.

In *A Court of Thorns and Roses*, Feyre is afraid Tamlin will never be able to take off his mask. She is also afraid she is not enough for Tamlin.

In *Legendborn*, Bree is afraid of Sel. She is also afraid of who she is.

In *A Game of Thrones*, Eddard is afraid for his daughters. He is also afraid of who he is.

Your Fun Task

Actions

For Outlining:

Create the main event for the reaction to the external middle plot point and add it to your fantasy vault.

For Editing:

In one to two sentences, summarize the main event for the reaction to the external middle plot point and add it to your fantasy vault.

Decisions

While outlining, make the following decisions and add them to your fantasy vault:

- How will you show the protagonist being proactive instead of reactive?

- What will the protagonist be afraid of?
- Will their fear be internal, external, or both?

Checklist

○ Show what the protagonist is afraid of externally.

○ Show what the protagonist is afraid of internally.

Chapter Twenty-Nine: Lead-Up to the Supernatural Middle Plot Point

The purpose of this scene is to make the supernatural middle plot point believable by showing the protagonist recognizing they are missing trust from their life. Not trusting others means decisions are risky.

The protagonist will be the POV character for the upcoming supernatural middle plot point, which means they must be in this scene if it's going to influence their behavior. You get to choose which character is the POV character for this scene.

This scene must come before the supernatural middle plot point, but it doesn't have to be directly before the scene. There can be other scenes between this scene and the supernatural middle plot point.

Example Novels: Lead-Up to the Supernatural Middle Plot Point

Fourth Wing by Rebecca Yarros

Violet stands up to Jack, Dain, and Xaden, showing Tairn and Andarna she's ready to channel their dragon powers. When Andarna channels her power to Violet and stops time in the supernatural middle plot point, the reader believes it's possible.

Twilight by Stephenie Meyer

Edward tells Bella he must go hunting. Drinking the blood of animals will reduce his hunger for her blood. This is preparation for the supernatural middle plot point. There is nothing scarier to Bella than not being with Edward. She knows the next day is pivotal. She's choosing to leave her world of humans. Bella lies to her dad and says she won't be with Edward. She has nobody she can trust to tell she is going with Edward because she knows if things go wrong, Edward will be in danger.

The Unbroken by C. L. Clark

Touraine sees a soft side of Princess Luca as Luca cares for the royal guard who was wounded by the crocodile. She wonders if the Shālan magic would help the guard but cannot share this idea with Luca. She doesn't trust Luca yet. This makes the supernatural middle plot point believable.

A Court of Thorns and Roses by Sarah J. Maas

Tamlin gives Feyre roses. She pretends they mean nothing but takes care of them. This shows the reader that she doesn't trust him enough to share her feelings. This sets up her emotional state for the supernatural middle plot point.

Legendborn by Tracy Deonn

Patricia teaches Bree about her ancestors' history. She tells her about root magic and that every family practices differently. Patricia tells her enough so Bree will trust her in the supernatural middle plot point when she wants to show Bree specific past events through dreams.

A Game of Thrones by George R. R. Martin

Daenerys tries to make peace between her brother and Drogo. She fails, which means she'll have to choose between Drogo and her brother. This makes the supernatural middle plot point where Daenerys hits her brother believable.

Lead-Up to the Supernatural Middle Plot Point Patterns

The protagonist shows they don't trust others, or they are not trusted, and they understand by the action in this scene that they will need to do something about it. All scenes show an event that makes the supernatural middle plot point believable.

> Violet stands up to Jack, Dain, and Xaden, showing Tairn and Andarna she's ready to channel their dragon powers. She hasn't received her dragon powers yet, and the main event in the scene shows she recognizes the need to prove she is strong enough. She needs the dragons to trust her.

> Bella chooses to leave the world of the humans by lying to her dad. When Bella lies, it shows she understands she can't live in the human world *and* be with Edward. This makes the next scene believable, she shows she doesn't trust humans, as she lies to her father and her friends.

> Touraine sees a side of Princess Luca that makes her look at her own abilities, and with all her Sand training, she realizes she has kept her mouth shut about using the healing for the guard who lost her leg. Touraine is missing both the ability to heal and to trust Luca. She wants to

change that because she sees how caring Luca is for someone who is no longer of value to her. Touraine becomes open to the idea of trusting Luca.

Patricia gives Bree enough information about her past to make Bree trust her. Bree understands she is missing knowledge so is willing to trust the information she receives.

Daenerys fails at making peace between her brother and Drogo and knows she'll have to choose between the two. She trusts her instincts and chooses Drogo.

Your Fun Task

Actions

For Outlining:

Create the main event for the lead-up to the supernatural middle plot point and add it to your fantasy vault.

For Editing:

In one to two sentences, summarize the main event for the lead-up to the supernatural middle plot point and add it to your fantasy vault.

Decision

While outlining, make the following decision and add it to your fantasy vault:

- Will the protagonist lack trust in themselves or in another character?

Checklist

○ Show an event that makes the upcoming supernatural middle plot point believable.

○ The protagonist is in this scene.

○ The scene occurs before the supernatural middle plot point.

○ Show the protagonist is missing trust from their life.

Chapter Thirty: Supernatural Middle Plot Point

To create a strong supernatural middle plot point, try to include some of these things:

- The protagonist learns something critical about the supernatural.

- The protagonist engages with or drives the supernatural storyline forward.

- The protagonist makes a risky decision related to the supernatural and changes the story's direction.

The first two events cause the protagonist to make a risky decision. The risky decision, just like a false victory or defeat, can help or hinder the protagonist in reaching their supernatural story goal.

Example Novels: Supernatural Middle Plot Point

Fourth Wing by Rebecca Yarros

This scene is written over two chapters.

Violet is attacked while she is sleeping. Tairn uses telepathy to wake Violet. Violet channels Andarna and stops time. The first chapter in the supernatural middle plot point ends here.

In the next chapter, Violet understands it was Andarna who stopped time. Xaden kills all those who tried to kill Violet. Violet is surprised that she is alive. Xaden reads her mind, but she doesn't realize it. She goes into shock and Xaden helps her through it.

Twilight by Stephenie Meyer

The supernatural in this novel is Bella and her interaction with vampires.

Two scenes before the supernatural middle plot point, Edward tells Bella must leave to hunt. He must drink bloods so he's not hungry for hers.

In the supernatural middle plot point, Bella sees Edward's true power. He shows her what he looks like in the sunlight. She decides she'll risk death to be with him.

The Unbroken by C. L. Clark

Princess Luca tells Touraine she would do anything to help her people. This is in reaction to the lead-up to the supernatural middle plot point where one of Luca's guards loses her leg. Luca wishes she had the healing magic, so the guard could still have her leg, and Touraine decides to trust Luca and tell her the magic is real. Touraine learns she would do anything to keep the Sands alive.

This leads Touraine to change her course and broker a deal between Princess Luca and the rebels.

A Court of Thorns and Roses by Sarah J. Maas

Using magic, Tamlin shortens a table, and it takes all his energy. Feyre sees for the first time how much trouble they are in. This shows how the masks are limiting his magic. This is a false defeat because Feyre doesn't know Rhysand (High Fae) will help her break the ancient curse (her supernatural goal) with his magic.

Legendborn by Tracy Deonn

Bree is shown her history through dreams. She learns root magic is to protect them from others who want to harm them and to heal them when they are hurt. She learns she can see root magic and others can't. She sees Sel's ancestors. She also sees Hellhounds entering the human world twenty-five years ago. Bree learns she has more power than Patricia. Bree gets proactive in sharing who Sel really is and trusts William with the truth about Sel.

A Game of Thrones by George R. R. Martin

Daenerys hits her brother and threatens him with death. She is becoming proactive. She hugs dragon eggs and feels her baby move in her stomach. She uses dragon eggs for strength. Daenerys decides her baby is the true dragon and not her brother.

Supernatural Middle Plot Point Patterns

All protagonists learn something about the supernatural.

- Violet learns a young dragon can gift power to a human.

- Bella learns what Edward's true powers are.

- Touraine learns she would betray the keepers of magic to keep her Sands alive.

- Feyre learns how weak Tamlin's powers are.

- Bree learns how Sel was created and what he is.

- Daenerys learns her brother is not the dragon.

All protagonists engage with the supernatural.

- Violet uses Andarna's power to stay alive.

- Bella experiences Edward's supernatural powers.

- Touraine shares a critical secret about magic with Princess Luca.

- Feyre witnesses Tamlin using his magic.

- Bree uses root magic and discovers how Sel was created.

- Daenerys draws on strength from the dragon eggs to feel her unborn baby.

All protagonists make a risky decision related to the supernatural. These decisions are often related to trusting another character or themselves.

- Violet decides to trust Xaden with her secret about Andarna's power. This happens one scene later as a reaction to the supernatural middle plot point. Note that we are interested in the key functions being in the story and not strict about what scene that function occurs in.

- Bella decides to trust Edward and will risk death to be with him.

- Touraine decides to trust Luca and tell her the magic is real.

- Feyre decides to trust Tamlin and share her past with him.

- Bree decides to trust William with the truth about Sel.

- Daenerys trusts her instincts and decides her baby is the true dragon and not her brother.

Your Fun Task

Actions

For Outlining:

Create the main event for the supernatural middle plot point and add it to your fantasy vault.

For Editing:

In one or two sentences, summarize the main event for the supernatural middle plot point and add it to your fantasy vault.

Decision

While outlining, make the following decision and add it to your fantasy vault:

- Does this scene come before, after, or in the same scene as the external middle plot point?

Checklist

Ensure the scene covers some or all the items on this list.

- Show the protagonist learning something about the supernatural.

- Show the protagonist engaging with or driving the supernatural storyline forward.

- Show the protagonist making a risky decision that is related to the supernatural and changes the story's direction.

Chapter Thirty-One: Reaction to the Supernatural Middle Plot Point

The purpose of this scene is to show who the protagonist will trust. They may put their trust in the wrong character, and it's possible the trust is short-lived.

Example Novels: Reaction to the Supernatural Middle Plot Point

Fourth Wing by Rebecca Yarros

Violet learns stopping time is not her signet. It's the dragon giving her the power. A signet is a combination of the dragon's power and who the person is at the core of their being.

Xaden tells Violet that she didn't try to kill the attackers and needs to learn to kill.

Violet discovers that Xaden, his dragon, and her dragon can all communicate telepathically.

She decides to trust Xaden with her secret about Andarna's power.

This scene starts in the second half of the chapter that includes the supernatural middle plot point.

Twilight by Stephenie Meyer

Bella asks Edward intimate questions and he answers. Their relationship is going in a new direction. Edward trusts Bella, and she trusts him in return.

The Unbroken by C. L. Clark

Touraine goes to the rebels to negotiate the trade of one hundred guns in exchange for knowledge about the Brigāni magic. Touraine negotiates, trusting that Princess Luca will do everything she has promised. Touraine is desperate at the end of the scene to trust her mother. But she is dismissed, and told that she killed her uncle, and Touraine's mother wants nothing to do with her.

A Court of Thorns and Roses by Sarah J. Maas

Feyre and Tamlin spend the day in the glen getting to know each other. Tamlin removes his glamor and shows Feyre what he truly looks like. Feyre is starting to trust him with her heart and her well-being.

Legendborn by Tracy Deonn

Bree tells William, the healer, that Sel is a bloodcrafter and dangerous. Bloodcrafters let Hellhounds in the world twenty-five years ago. She thinks Sel is a Crossroads man, and she doesn't trust him. Bree shows she trusts William.

A Game of Thrones by George R. R. Martin

Right after Daenerys tells her unborn child he is the true dragon, she dreams of her home. She has not accepted the Dothraki as her home yet. She trusts her unborn son to give her strength.

The reaction to the supernatural middle plot point is the final sentence in the same scene that includes the lead-up to the supernatural middle plot point and the supernatural middle plot point.

Reaction to the Supernatural Middle Plot Point Patterns

In each of the scenes, the reaction of the protagonist is to trust another character. They need more than themselves to succeed in achieving their story goal.

Violet trusts Xaden.

Bella trusts Edward.

Touraine trusts Luca.

Feyre trusts Tamlin.

Bree trusts William.

Daenerys trusts her unborn son.

Your Fun Task

Actions

For Outlining:

Create the main event for the supernatural reaction to the middle plot point and add it to your fantasy vault.

For Editing:

In one to two sentences, summarize the main event for the supernatural reaction to the middle plot point and add it to your fantasy vault.

Decision

While outlining, make the following decision and add it to your fantasy vault:

- Which character will the protagonist trust?

Checklist

  ○ Show the protagonist trusting another character.

Chapter Thirty-Two: External Pressures

These are external pressures that make it hard for the protagonist to achieve their external or supernatural goal. The external pressures come from the actions of other characters.

There are many types of external pressures which can be shown in any order in your story. Here are some ideas for you.

The actions of others:

1. Impede the protagonist's path to the story goal.
2. Force the protagonist to make a choice.
3. Reveal a major new insight and change how the protagonist sees the story goal.

The actions of others can be in the scene itself or it can be something that has happened before this scene starts.

If the external and supernatural come together in the middle plot point, then these external pressures can be in the same scenes for each plot line, but they don't have to be. This is your artistic decision.

Example Novels: External Pressures

Fourth Wing by Rebecca Yarros

The actions of other characters reveal a major new insight and change how the Violet sees the story goal. Violet's mother wants to study Andarna because she's a golden dragon and rare. Violet knows she must protect her dragon and keep her safe from her mother. This adds additional pressure because she can't just focus on training and getting her signet. This makes it harder for Violet to achieve both the supernatural and the external story goals.

The actions of others force Violet to make a choice. After Violet has broken into her mother's office, Violet reads her mother's letter about the situation outside the wards, and it's proof the leaders are hiding something. Violet feels pressured because she can't trust those who are leading them into battle. She is choosing herself over her mother.

The actions of other characters impede the path to the story goal. Violet's sister and Xaden keep Violet from fighting when gryphons arrive. Violet can't save Navarre if she can't fight.

Twilight by Stephenie Meyer

The actions of other characters impede the path to the story goal. Jacob and Billy are waiting at Bella's home when Edward drops her off. They don't want Bella spending time with Edward. This is additional pressure because she can't focus on her relationship with Edward. She must keep Jacob and Billy from interfering.

The actions of others force the protagonist to make a choice. Bella's dad asks her about boys. He's watching her more closely, and this makes it hard for her to spend time with Edward. She is choosing Edward over her dad. The first half of this scene contains both the main event for the external pressure 3 scene, and the second half contains the main event for the lead-up to plot point 2.

The Unbroken by C. L. Clark

The actions of other characters impede the path to the story goal. Touraine meets the Many Legged. She learns she'll need their agreement if they want help fighting the Balladairans across the sea. Touraine understands the Many Legged also took Guiren's leg when they attacked Touraine and Princess Luca while they were looking for a book on magic. This is additional pressure because Touraine now has an additional group to negotiate with.

The actions of others force Touraine to make a choice. Touraine is pressured by Princess Luca to get her the healing magic. If Luca doesn't get power away from her uncle, there will be a civil war that will kill many Sands. Touraine and Luca fight about how to proceed and Touraine chooses to side with the rebels instead of Luca.

The actions of other characters reveal a major new insight and change how Touraine sees the story goal. Touraine's mother tells her she no longer loves her. Touraine is trying to be part of the rebels, and this makes it difficult.

A Court of Thorns and Roses by Sarah J. Maas

The actions of other characters reveal a major new insight and change how Feyre sees the story goal. Feyre wakes to see Alis as she truly looks. Her glamor has been removed. She can now see the fairies that Tamlin has been hiding from her. Tamlin is worried about her safety because the blight is growing. This puts pressure on Feyre to help the fairies.

The actions of others force the protagonist to make a choice. Lucien informs Tamlin the blight took two dozen younglings. It burned their magic and blew their minds apart. The house goes silent because another mythical creature arrives, so Lucien hides Feyre. Rhysand appears and finds Feyre. His magic takes over, and he reaches into her mind. This is a critical moment in the series and in book one. Tamlin begs Rhysand not to tell Amarantha (the evil one who created the curse) about him and Feyre.

Rhysand demands she give her name. She gives him a fake name: Claire Beddor. This puts external pressure on Feyre because she sees no way she can fight against Rhysand.

Feyre chooses Tamlin over Rhysand.

The actions of other characters impede the path to the external story goal. In the previous scene, Feyre discovers Claire Beddor's family was killed and their house burned to the ground. Claire is the name she gave Rhysand. Feyre decides she's going back to Prythian and tells her family about the dangers they face. On her return, she travels to Tamlin's and finds his home empty. This provides additional pressure. She thought she was going back to work with him to save his kind. Now, she has to save him and his kind on her own.

Legendborn by Tracy Deonn

The actions of other characters reveal a major new insight and change how Bree sees the story goal. The second trial from Sel is a scavenger hunt. Bree is competing to stay in the Order and must perform well. Only eight Pages remain in the running. The pressure is exerted because the more ether objects they collect in the scavenger hunt, the more the Hellhounds are attracted to them. She risks death to do well in the scavenger hunt, but she must win if she wants to stay in the Order. This puts pressure on Bree because she has to focus on the task and not on finding out who killed her mother.

The actions of others force Bree to make a choice. Her mentor Patricia tells her she must keep her abilities secret from the Order, or she'll be in danger. Bree is stuck between Root magic and the Order. Bree decides she is her family's Scion. She chooses her family over the Order.

The actions of other characters impede the path to the external story goal. The third challenge the Pages must face is combat trial. Bree has less strength and control of her magic than the others, so this adds pressure and makes it hard for her to reach her story goal.

A Game of Thrones by George R. R. Martin

The actions of other characters reveal a major new insight and change how Daenerys sees the story goal. A wine seller tries to poison Daenerys. Jorah saves her but only because he knows there is poison in the wine. She now understands people are actively trying to kill her. For help, she puts the dragon eggs in a fire, but nothing happens. She wants more strength from them. This puts additional pressure on Daenerys because she doesn't know who she is safe with.

The actions of others force the protagonist to make a choice. Catelyn learns Sansa is a hostage at King's Landing. She no longer has Tyrion to trade for her daughters. This puts pressure on the Stark family. In plot point 2, Eddard won't admit to treason or ask Robb to stand down with his army. This puts Sansa's life in danger, and they have no leverage with Tyrion as a hostage. Catelyn chooses family over the kingdom. Eddard will choose the kingdom over family, putting Catelyn and Eddard in conflict.

The actions of other characters impede the path to the external story goal. Tyrion's father forces him to go to war. He is not built for fighting. His skill is negotiating, and he can't use this in battle. This puts pressure on Tyrion, and by extension, the humans because he can't use his natural skills to win the throne.

External Pressures Patterns

Impede the protagonist's path to the story goal.

> Violet's sister and Xaden keep Violet from fighting when gryphons arrive. Violet can't save Navarre if she can't fight.

Jacob and Billy are waiting at Bella's home when Edward drops her off. They don't want Bella spending time with Edward.

Touraine meets the Many Legged. She learns she'll need their agreement if they want help fighting the Balladairans across the sea.

Feyre travels to Tamlin's and finds his home empty.

The third challenge Bree must face is combat trial.

Tyrion's father forces him to go to war. He is not built for fighting. His skill is negotiating, and he can't use this in battle

Force the protagonist to make a choice.

Violet chooses herself over her mother.

Bella chooses Edward over her dad.

Touraine chooses to side with the rebels instead of Luca.

Feyre chooses Tamlin over Rhysand.

Bree chooses her family over the Order.

Catelyn chooses family over the kingdom. Eddard chooses the kingdom over family.

Reveal a major new insight and change how the protagonist sees the story goal.

Violet knows she must protect her dragon and keep her safe from her mother.

Touraine tries to be part of the rebels instead of her army.

Feyre now wants to help the fairies instead of only trying to get home.

Bree focuses on the task and not on finding out who killed her mother.

Daenerys understands people are actively trying to kill her.

Your Fun Task

Actions

For Outlining:

Create the main event for the external pressures and add it to your fantasy vault. Try to have at least three unique external pressures.

In the order that best suits your outline add:

1. A scene where the main event has the actions of others impeding the protagonist's path to the story goal.
2. A scene where the main event has the action of others forces the protagonist to make a choice.
3. A scene where the main event reveals a major new insight and changes how the protagonist sees the story goal.

For Editing:

In one to two sentences, summarize the main event for the three external pressures and add it to your fantasy vault. These can be in any order.

1. Find the scene where the actions of others impede the protagonist's path to the story goal.
2. Find the scene where the actions of others force the protagonist to make a choice.
3. Find the scene where the actions of others reveal a major new insight and change how the protagonist sees the story goal.

If there are not at least three external pressures, try writing a new scene with a unique external pressure.

Decisions

While outlining, make the following decisions and add them to your fantasy vault:

- How will each external pressure make it hard for the protagonist to achieve the story goal?

- Which order will the scenes be presented to the reader?

- Will there be a set of scenes for both story goals, or will they be connected in one scene?

Checklist

○ Show the protagonist being distracted from their external or supernatural story goal.

○ Show an external pressure impeding the protagonist's path to the story goal.

○ Show an external pressure forcing the protagonist to make a choice.

○ Show an external pressure revealing a major new insight and changing how the protagonist sees the story goal.

Chapter Thirty-Three: Lead-Up to the External Plot Point 2

The purpose of this scene is to show the protagonist preparing for the external plot point 2. Often this means they are preparing to protect others, or that others are protecting the protagonist, or that they cannot provide the protection they desperately want to give.

This scene should make the main event in the external plot point 2 painful. The main event in this scene can remind the reader of what the protagonist has to lose.

Example Novels: Lead-Up to the External Plot Point 2

Fourth Wing by Rebecca Yarros

Xaden has a saddle made for Violet because she can't stay on her dragon. Tairn has to use magic to keep her on his back, and that tires him. Violet won't be able to fight properly if she can't stay mounted.

By giving Violet the gift of a saddle, Xaden is preparing her for plot point 2 where she has to fight in the school's war games. Violet knows if she dies, so does Xaden. She has more to lose than just herself, and Xaden is protecting her.

Twilight by Stephenie Meyer

Bella goes home to prepare her father for her departure. She lies to him and says she broke up with Edward and is going back to Phoenix to be with her mother. She's doing this to protect him from the evil vampires.

The Unbroken by C. L. Clark

Touraine tries to help those who are wounded in an attack. Her mother finds her and tells her to leave. Touraine wants to prepare for battle, and her mother scoffs at her. Still, Touraine will protect herself by getting ready to face her enemies.

A Court of Thorns and Roses by Sarah J. Maas

Feyre has traveled from Tamlin's home to the underground cave where he's being held. She enters the cave and meets an Attor. She knows she will be killed but has to save Tamlin. This is her first view of how dangerous saving Tamlin will be. She's preparing to protect him.

Legendborn by Tracy Deonn

Bree's father gives her mother's necklace to her. He tells her to make her life about love and not loss. Her father is preparing her for her future.

A Game of Thrones by George R. R. Martin

The scene opens with Eddard in jail. He has been arrested for treason, and his future looks hopeless. With King Robert dead and Joffrey as the new king, he's lost his ally. He thinks of his daughters and forces himself not to cry and his death is coming. He is mentally preparing himself for death and knows his honor cannot protect his children

Lead-Up to the External Plot Point 2: Patterns

Each scene shows a preparation of some type.

In *First Wing*, Xaden helps Violet prepare for the upcoming battle by giving her a dragon saddle.

In *Twilight*, Bella prepares her father for her departure.

In *The Unbroken*, Touraine wants to prepare for battle and her mother scoffs at her.

In *A Court of Thorns and Roses*, Feyre wants to protect Tamlin.

In *Legendborn*, Bree's father gives her a necklace to help prepare her for the future.

In *A Game of Thrones,* Eddard prepares to die.

The protagonists or another character in the six examples all prepare to protect someone or something.

In *First Wing*, Xaden helps Violet prepare for the upcoming battle by giving her a dragon saddle. This is to protect her, and therefore himself, as they are connected by the mated dragons.

In *Twilight*, Bella prepares her father for her departure. She lies to her father to protect him from the truth about vampires.

In *The Unbroken*, Touraine wants to protect herself by preparing for battle.

In *A Court of Thorns and Roses,* by entering the cave, Feyre wants to protect the fairy she loves.

In *Legendborn,* Bree's father gives her a necklace to help protect her in the future.

In *A Game of Thrones,* Eddard prepares to die. He wants to protect the truth at the cost of not only his own life but of his children.

Your Fun Task

Actions

For Outlining:

Create the main event for the lead-up to the external plot point 2 and add it to your fantasy vault.

For Editing:

In one to two sentences, summarize the main event for the lead-up to the external plot point 2 and add it to your fantasy vault.

Decisions

While outlining, make the following decisions and add them to your fantasy vault:

- Who is the protagonist trying to protect?
- Or is someone trying to protect the protagonist?

Checklist

- Show the protagonist or another character preparing to protect someone or something.

Chapter Thirty-Four: External Plot Point 2

The protagonist gets the final piece of information they need to address the external story goal in the climax scene.

Plot point 2 is an emotional low point for your protagonist. The actions they've taken since the middle plot point have caused a disaster, and they don't know if they can recover. More importantly, the readers worry the protagonist won't recover. It marks a turning point in the story.

Plot point 2 should:

1. Be told from the protagonist's point of view.
2. Be written in active form.
3. Cause the protagonist to be at their lowest emotional point of the story so far.
4. Share the final piece of information the protagonist needs to address the external goal.
5. Create a sense of urgency.
6. Mirror plot point 1.

Example Novels: External Plot Point 2

Fourth Wing by Rebecca Yarros

Violet faces dark forces. She learns she can use lightning when she kills Jack. This is her first time killing another and is her lowest moment in the story.

This scene is also the supernatural plot point 2. Violet uses lightning to kill Jack, but she can't control it. She learns lightning is her signet and that she can kill someone. This is the knowledge she needs for the climax scene.

She also realizes she must quickly learn to control her lightning, or she may accidentally kill others.

In the external plot point 1, Violet uses poison to weaken her opponents but not kill them. Here, Violet uses lightning to kill Jack. The mirror occurs because in one scene Violet wins without killing and in the external plot point 2, she wins by killing.

Twilight by Stephenie Meyer

The Cullen family make a plan for Bella to leave with Alice (Edward's sister). Edward and his brother stay to face the vampire tracker.

Bella and Edward split up, and this is devastating to Bella. Edward and his brothers lure the tracker. Edward's sisters take Bella south. Bella's external goal is to make a life in Forks and now she is leaving it.

All the Cullens protect Bella. She learns the Cullens are more important to her than her own life. This is the information she needs to address the external climax and stay in Forks.

This is her lowest point because she knows she's the cause of all the pain and danger.

In the external plot point 1, Bella tells her mother she is staying in Forks with Edward. In the external plot point 2, she leaves Edward and Forks. You can see the mirror with staying and leaving.

The Unbroken by C. L. Clark

Touraine can't go back to being a Sand and she can't go to Princess Luca. She fights with her mother and punches her in the jaw. This is the lowest point for Touraine because she belongs nowhere. She contemplates suicide and then decides to die fighting. She learns she wants to die for a reason, and this is the information she needs to fight in the climax scene.

In the external plot point 1, Touraine chose a job with Princess Luca instead of death. The mirror occurs because in the external plot point 1, the choice of life or death is given to Touraine, and she chooses life. In the external plot point 2, she chooses death.

A Court of Thorns and Roses by Sarah J. Maas

Instead of killing Feyre, an Attor takes her to Amarantha (the evil fairy). Tamlin is sitting beside Amarantha and ignores Feyre.

Feyre learns Claire was tortured before she died. She gave Claire's name to Rhysand and now knows she not only caused her death, but she caused her to be tortured too. This is Feyre's low point in the novel.

Feyre tells Amarantha she's come to claim the one she loves (Tamlin). Amarantha says Feyre must complete the tasks for the spell on Tamlin and the other High Fae to be broken. Amarantha also gives her a riddle, and this is the information she needs to win at the climax. Amarantha is the dark force that Feyre must face.

Earlier in the story, Feyre couldn't read yet. She went to the library to learn more about the curse. In this scene, she is standing in front of the woman who issued the curse. In both scenes she is acting to save Tamlin's life.

In plot point 1, Feyre stole a knife. She decided she made a promise to her mother to take care of her sisters and she was going to keep that promise. This scene mirrors plot point 1 because she is won't take care of her family, she's going to take care of Tamlin's family.

Legendborn by Tracy Deonn

Bree finds out her mother hid from the Order and from her. By digging into her mother's past, she is undoing all the good her mother did. She learns that no matter how her mother died, she still feels incredible pain. Bree learns of the family curse and Bloodcraft. Only one daughter at a time can have Bloodcraft. This is her lowest moment.

In the external plot point 1, Bree took the oath so she could stay inside of the Order and find out who killed her mother. In this scene, understanding this won't help her heal. The mirror occurs because Bree thinks she can heal in plot point 1 and knows she can't in plot point 2.

A Game of Thrones by George R. R. Martin

Varys visits Eddard in Jail. He asks Eddard to admit to treason and instruct Robb to lay down his arms. Eddard refuses. Varys warns him Sansa will suffer because of his actions. The Lannisters are the dark forces Eddard will have to face.

Eddard fails to achieve his external story goal, and so he doesn't receive the final piece of information he needs.

In the external plot point 1, Eddard and Catelyn make a plan to protect the North if war breaks out. In plot point 2, Eddard can't protect anyone. Knowing he can't protect his family is a fate worse than death. This is his lowest moment even though he is executed in the external climax.

External Plot Point 2 Patterns

Each protagonist learns something:

In *Fourth Wing*, Violet learns she must control her lightning, or she will kill innocent people.

In *Twilight*, Bella learns the Cullens are more important to her than her own life.

In *The Unbroken*, Touraine learns she wants to die for a reason.

In *A Court of Thorns and Roses*, Feyre learns her friend Claire was tortured before she died.

In *Legendborn*, Bree learns of the family curse and Bloodcraft. Only one daughter at a time can have Bloodcraft. When the daughter gets it, the mother dies.

In *A Game of Thrones*, Eddard learns he cannot protect his family.

Your Fun Task

Actions

For Outlining:

Create the main event for the external plot point 2 and add it to your fantasy vault.

For Editing:

In one to two sentences, summarize the main event for external plot point 2 and add it to your fantasy vault.

Decisions

While outlining, make the following decisions and add them to your fantasy vault:

- What does the protagonist learn?
- What dark forces do they face?

Checklist

- Show the protagonist learning something that will help or hinder them in the climax scene.
- Write from the protagonist's point of view.
- Write in active form.

- Cause the protagonist to be at their lowest emotional point of the story so far.

- Share the final piece of information the protagonist needs to address the story goal.

- Create a sense of urgency.

- Mirror plot point 1.

Chapter Thirty-Five: Reaction to the External Plot Point 2

The purpose of this scene in a fantasy novel is to show the protagonist choosing between or connecting two groups.

The reader must see the protagonist's reaction to the lowest point in the story.

The main event can show what the protagonist intends to do with the final piece of information they received.

Example Novels: Reaction to the External Plot Point 2

The Fourth Wing by Rebecca Yarros

Violet has killed Jack and has to live with that. Up to now, she tried not to be a killer. The Fourth Wing won. Dain says Violet doesn't have to use her power. Xaden tells him to stay away from her. Violet cannot connect Dain and Xaden and chooses Xaden's side.

Twilight by Stephenie Meyer

Bella hides in a hotel with Edward's siblings. She is frightened for Edward. She chooses to keep the evil and good vampires apart.

The Unbroken by C. L. Clark

Touraine is done negotiating and trusting Princess Luca. She reveals General Cantic only knew about half of the gun supply. They have more guns to fight and decide to fight to the death. She chooses the rebellion over the Sands and Princess Luca.

A Court of Thorns and Roses by Sarah J. Maas

Feyre wakes up in a prison cell. She has been badly beaten. Lucien visits and heals her nose. She learns she must work with him if she is going to succeed. Amarantha has brought all the high lords under the mountain, and they can't leave until Feyre's trial is over. She knows she will die. She has chosen death with the fairies over life with the humans.

Legendborn by Tracy Deonn

Bree contacts Patricia. She wants to speak to her ancestors about Bloodcraft. She connects with her deceased grandmother first but wants to go farther back in time. Bree wants to connect the women in her past and the present.

A Game of Thrones by George R. R. Martin

Eddard begs Varys not to hurt Sansa because she is just a child. Eddard tries to get Tyrion to ignore that the Lannisters and Starks are enemies and bring the two families together enough to protect Sansa. Varys reminds him of other children that were killed in the battle for a throne. Varys gives him a choice between having the next person to visit him give him an easy way to kill himself, or they bring him Sansa's head. Eddard cannot connect the Lannisters and the Starks.

Reaction to the External Plot Point 2 Patterns

This scene is about connecting two groups of people or choosing between two groups.

In *Fourth Wing*, Violet chooses between Dain and Xaden.

In *Twilight*, Bella chooses to hide her plans and to keep the evil and good vampires apart.

In *The Unbroken*, Touraine chooses the rebels over Princess Luca and the Sands army.

In *A Game of Thorns and Roses*, Feyre chooses death with the fairies over life with the humans.

In *Legendborn*, Bree wants to connect the women in her past and the present.

In *A Game of Thrones*, Eddard tried to get Tyrion to ignore that the Lannisters and Starks are enemies and bring the two families together enough to protect Sansa.

Your Fun Task

Actions

For Outlining:

Create the main event for the reaction to the external plot point 2 and add it to your fantasy vault.

For Editing:

In one to two sentences, summarize the main event for reaction to external plot point 2 and add it to your fantasy vault.

Decision

While outlining, make the following decision and add it to your fantasy vault:

- Will the protagonist choose between two groups, or will they connect two groups?

Checklist

○ Show the protagonist choosing between two groups or connecting two groups.

Chapter Thirty-Six: Lead-Up to the Supernatural Plot Point 2

The protagonist learns something about another character that shows if they must work with that character in the climax or not. The scene shows whether the protagonist can or can't trust the character. The information they learn is critical for the protagonist to address the supernatural story goal in the climax scene.

Example Novels: Lead-Up to the Supernatural Plot Point 2

The Fourth Wing by Rebecca Yarros

Xaden has a saddle made for Violet because she can't stay on her dragon. Violet understands Xaden is helping her. This is the motivation she needs to trust him during the final battle. Trusting him is the right decision for Violet.

Twilight by Stephenie Meyer

Bella attends a baseball game with Edward and his family. She understands the closeness in Edward's family and this shows us what she has to lose if she can't become part of it. This is the motivation she needs to face the climax scene alone. She doesn't trust the Cullens enough to let them save her. This is the reason Edward has to save her from the evil vampire. Not trusting the Cullens is the wrong decision for Bella.

The Unbroken by C. L. Clark

The priestess's wife teaches Touraine about the tenets of the Shālan magic. The magic requires flesh to mend flesh, hence the need to eat meat. Touraine asks the priestess's wife to teach her how to pray. This is the motivation she needs to use magic in the climax. Trusting the priestess is the right decision.

A Court of Thorns and Roses by Sarah J. Maas

Rhysand visits Feyre in her cell. He reminds her that if she fails the tasks, Amarantha will continue to rule. She decides to trust Rhysand, and it's the right decision.

Legendborn by Tracy Deonn

Bree attends the ceremony. She feels Sel's connection to her without seeing him and gasps when the connection is gone. The breaking of the connection with Sel is the motivation she needs to trust him during the final battle. This is the right decision.

A Game of Thrones by George R. R. Martin

Drogo's wound has festered. Daenerys knows she must do something drastic to save him. This gives her the motivation to make a deal with the Maegi. She trusts the Maegi, and this is the wrong decision.

Lead-Up to the Supernatural Plot Point 2 Patterns

In *Fourth Wing*, Violet understands Xaden is helping her and trusts him.

In *Twilight,* Bella doesn't trust the Cullens' abilities and thinks she has to act alone in the climax scene.

In the *Unbroken*, Touraine trusts the priestess, and this is the motivation she needs to use magic in the climax.

In *A Court of Thorns and Roses*, Feyre trusts Rhysand and he helps her survive the three tasks.

In *Legendborn,* Bree's connection with Sel is the motivation she needs to trust him during the final battle.

In *A Game of Thrones,* Daenerys trusts the Maegi, and this decision kills her son.

Your Fun Task

Actions

For Outlining:

Create the main event for the lead-up to the supernatural plot point 2 and add it to your fantasy vault.

For Editing:

In one to two sentences, summarize the main event for the lead-up to supernatural plot point 2 and add it to your fantasy vault.

Decision

While outlining, make the following decision and add it to your fantasy vault:

- What does the protagonist learn about another character that enables them to trust that character?

Checklist

○ Show the protagonist trusting another character regarding something that is critical in the climax scene.

Chapter Thirty-Seven: Supernatural Plot Point 2

The protagonist gains knowledge about the supernatural that they can use in the climax, and they face a first major limitation of the supernatural.

There must be a limitation to the supernatural or the reader will know the protagonist will succeed. This limitation is going to make success difficult in the climax.

Example Novels: Supernatural Plot Point 2

Fourth Wing by Rebecca Yarros

Violet learns lightning is her signet. She uses it to kill Jack, but she can't control it. Violet learns the power of her magic. She also learns magic gives her the ability to kill. This is the knowledge she needs for the climax scene.

This is the last time Violet channels Andarna's ability to stop time. That magic cannot come back, so it's the end of that magic story arc.

Violet learns channeling her power through a dragon depletes both her energy and the dragons' energy. This is the supernatural limitation.

This is the same scene as the external plot point 2.

Twilight by Stephenie Meyer

A group of evil vampires arrives at the Cullen's baseball game. They realize Bella is human, and an evil vampire tracker desires her blood. Edward protects her from the dark forces but shows the limitations of their powers. Bella learns the Cullens aren't as powerful as she thought.

The Unbroken by C. L. Clark

The priestess's wife teaches Touraine about the tenets of the Shālan magic. The magic requires flesh to mend flesh, hence the need to eat meat. Touraine asks the priestess's wife to teach her how to pray.

They have a quiet moment together helping the sick. This will make it more painful for Touraine when Captain Rogan arrests the priestess's wife.

This occurs before the external plot point 2.

A Court of Thorns and Roses by Sarah J. Maas

Feyre must kill three High Fae. This is her lowest moment in the supernatural because she kills two innocent High Fae. Because she is not High Fae yet, she can't use magic to win. This is her limitation. Feyre learns she can kill innocent fairies to protect the larger group.

Legendborn by Tracy Deonn

Bree accepts Nick's offer to be his squire. The room erupts in hatred for Bree. Bree learns no matter what title she is given, others will hate her because she is different from them. The power received by becoming Nick's squire isn't strong enough to protect her.

A Game of Thrones by George R. R. Martin

Daenerys makes a deal with Maegi to save Drogos' life. The deal is that she must trade one life for another. She cannot get the Maegi to save Drogo's life without the exchange. Daenerys learns her powers as Khaleesi are limited.

Supernatural Plot Point 2 Patterns

Each protagonist learns something.

> Violet learns lightning is her signet.
>
> Bella learns the Cullens aren't as powerful as she thought.
>
> Touraine learns the tenets of the Shālan magic.
>
> Feyre learns she can kill innocent fairies to protect the larger group.
>
> Bree learns no matter what title she is given, others will hate her because she is different from them.
>
> Daenerys learns her powers as Khaleesi are limited.

Your Fun Task

Actions

For Outlining:

Create the main event for the supernatural plot point 2 and add it to your fantasy vault.

For Editing:

In one to two sentences, summarize the main event for the supernatural plot point 2 and add it to your fantasy vault.

Decision

While outlining, make the following decision and add it to your fantasy vault:

- What knowledge does the protagonist gain about the supernatural?

Checklist

○ Show the protagonist gaining knowledge about the supernatural that they can use in the climax.

○ Show the protagonist facing the first major limitation of the supernatural.

Chapter Thirty-Eight: Reaction to the Supernatural Plot Point 2

The purpose of the reaction to the supernatural plot point 2 is to show the protagonist in a worse state than before the scene.

Example Novels: Reaction to the Supernatural Plot Point 2

Fourth Wing by Rebecca Yarros

Violet has killed Jack and has to live with that. Dain says Violet doesn't have to use her power. Xaden tells him to stay away from her. Violet believes she traded Liam's life for Jack's and that keeps the gods in balance. She also believes she is broken forever because she killed Jack. She is better off because she has her signet, but worse off because she understands her signet is meant to kill.

This is also the reaction to the external plot point 2.

Twilight by Stephenie Meyer

The Cullens and Bella run from the evil vampires. Bella is not strong enough to influence the plan to survive. The Cullens make a plan and expect Bella to follow it. She is worse off because she is being isolated from Edward.

The Unbroken by C. L. Clark

The priestess's wife is taken by Captain Rogan, and Touraine thinks it's her fault. She is worse off because she has failed to help others.

A Court of Thorns and Roses by Sarah J. Maas

Tamlin is weakened from being stabbed by Feyre and can't attack Amarantha. Amarantha refuses to lift the curse because she never said when she would lift it. Feyre realizes her mistake, and that she has not won. She is worse off because she failed to break the curse.

Legendborn by Tracy Deonn

Bree is kidnapped by Nick's father. She is worse off because her best friend is also kidnapped. Her actions have brought someone she loves in harm's way.

A Game of Thrones by George R. R. Martin

Daenerys' son dies, and she kills Drogo. She won't let Drogo live in a state where he can't be a warrior. She knows that's worse than death for him. She is worse off because she has lost two people she loves.

Reaction to Supernatural Plot Point 2 Patterns

Each of the six novels show the protagonist in a worse state than before the supernatural plot point 2.

Violet understands her signet is meant to kill.

Bella is isolated from Edward.

Touraine has failed to help others.

Feyre has failed to break the curse.

Bree's actions have brought someone she loves in harm's way.

Daenerys has lost two people she loves.

Your Fun Task

Actions

For Outlining:

Create the main event for the reaction to the supernatural plot point 2 and add it to your fantasy vault.

For Editing:

In one to two sentences, summarize the main event for the reaction to supernatural plot point 2 and add it to your fantasy vault.

Decision

While outlining, make the following decision and add it to your fantasy vault:

- Will the protagonist be worse off because they have harmed themselves or someone else?

Checklist

- Show the protagonist in a worse state than before the supernatural plot point 2.

Chapter Thirty-Nine: Protagonist Understands the Story Goal

The purpose of this scene is to show that the protagonist understands what they learned in plot point 2 and how this will help them achieve their story goal. The main event in this scene must build on what the protagonist learned in plot point 2 and the realization that happened in the reaction to plot point 2.

It's common for the protagonist to understand the story goal anywhere after plot point 2 up to the final climax scene. When the protagonist understands their true story goal, they will need the supernatural to achieve it.

Each protagonist learns something in both the external and supernatural plot point 2 scenes.

In the external plot point 2:

> Violet learns she must control her lightning or she will kill innocent people.

> Bella learns the Cullens are more important to her than her own life.

> Touraine learns she wants to die for a reason.

> Feyre learns her friend Claire was tortured before she died.

> Bree learns of the family curse and Bloodcraft. Only one daughter at a time can have Bloodcraft. When the daughter gets it, the mother dies.

Eddard learns he cannot protect his family.

In the supernatural plot point 2:

Violet learns lightning is her signet.

Bella learns the Cullens aren't as powerful as Bella thought.

Touraine learns the tenets of the Shālan magic.

Feyre learns she can kill innocent fairies to protect the larger group.

Bree learns no matter what title she is given, others will hate her because she is different from them.

Daenerys learns her powers as Khaleesi are limited.

Example Novels: Protagonist Understands the Story Goal

Fourth Wing by Rebecca Yarros

In the supernatural plot point 2, Violet learned she has to control her lightning, or she will kill innocent people. She understands her story goal is not just to live, it's living to protect innocent citizens. This comes right after they think they are participating in a war game and not a real war.

Twilight by Stephenie Meyer

In the external plot point 2, Bella learns the Cullens are more important to her than her own life. In the supernatural plot point 2, she learns the Cullens aren't as powerful as she thought. Both scenes help Bella understand she must die to protect those she loves. Her real supernatural story goal is not to live among vampires. It's dying for them, so they can live.

The Unbroken by C. L. Clark

In the external plot point 2, Touraine learns she wants to die for a reason. She will die for others. In the supernatural plot point 2, she learns the tenets of the Shālan magic. She understands her real external goal is to figure out who her people are.

A Court of Thorns and Roses by Sarah J. Maas

In the external plot point 2, Feyre learns her friend Claire was tortured before she died. In the supernatural plot point 2, she learns she can kill innocent fairies to protect the larger group. Feyre's initial external goal was to get home to her life with humans. She understands this was never her goal. It was to find a new home in Prythian.

Legendborn by Tracy Deonn

In the external plot point 2, Bree learns of the family curse and Bloodcraft. Only one daughter at a time can have Bloodcraft. When the daughter receives it, the mother dies. In the supernatural plot point 2, Bree learns no matter what title she is given, others will hate her because she is different from them.

Bree understands she will always be different. Right before the climax, she understands who she must become and that she will be different from everyone else.

A Game of Thrones by George R. R. Martin

In the external plot point 2, Eddard learns he cannot protect his family. In the supernatural plot point 2, Daenerys learns her powers as Khaleesi are limited.

Eddard doesn't need to understand the story goal as he dies in the external climax scene.

Daenerys understands that with her brother dead, she is the heir and the last blood of House Targaryen.

Protagonist Understands the Story Goal Patterns

Each of the protagonists alters either their external or supernatural story goal. Note that Bella in *Twilight* and Daenerys in *A Game of Thrones* change their supernatural goal. The others change their external goal.

> Violet changes her external story goal in order to make sure the stakes in the supernatural skeleton blurb never come to fruition. She understands her story goal is not just to live, it's living to protect innocent citizens.
>
> Bella changes her supernatural story goal. Her real supernatural story goal is not to live among vampires. It's dying for them so they can live.
>
> Touraine changes her external story goal. Her real external goal is to figure out who her people are.

Feyre changes her external story goal. Her real external goal is to find a new home in Prythian.

Bree changes her external story goal. Her real external goal is to find out the truth about who she is.

Daenerys changes her external story goal. Her real external goal is to rule all the kingdoms.

Your Fun Task

Actions

For Outlining:

Create the main event for the lead-up to the protagonist understands the story goal and add it to your fantasy vault.

For Editing:

In one to two sentences, summarize the main event for the protagonist understands the story goal and add it to your fantasy vault.

Decision

While outlining, make the following decision and add it to your fantasy vault:

- Which story goal will the protagonist alter?

Checklist

- Show the protagonist altering one of their story goals.

Chapter Forty: Lead-Up to the External Climax

The purpose of this scene is to show what the protagonist is giving up in order to achieve the external story goal during the climax. This raises the tension the reader feels for the upcoming climax.

Example Novels: Lead-Up to External Climax

Fourth Wing by Rebecca Yarros

Xaden is told to abandon the city under attack or abandon his command of the Fourth Wing. Venin attack the city and explode the gates.

Seven gryphons arrive to support Xaden and his team. Violet tells the team wyvern were created to compete with dragons and that venin channel power into them.

Violet sends Andarna to safety before the battle begins. Andarna won't abandon them.

Xaden gives them all a choice to leave or stay and fight. Violet knows this means death, and she chooses to stay.

This event occurs in the same scene as the lead-up to the supernatural climax.

Twilight by Stephenie Meyer

Bella and Edward are in the hospital, and they prepare what they are going to tell Bella's mother about why Edward is there. She's going to give up living with her mother so she can stay with Edward. This is a strong lead-up to Bella telling her mother why she will stay in Forks. Bella is giving up life with her mother.

The Unbroken by C. L. Clark

In the previous scene, Princess Luca offers to spare Touraine's life but not the lives of the other rebels. Touraine refuses and asks Luca to leave. Touraine tries to pray and fails. She still doesn't believe in gods or magic. She decides to die because she chooses to. The end is coming on her terms.

A Court of Thorns and Roses by Sarah J. Maas

Feyre's final task is to kill three fairies. She kills two. Tamlin is the third. She remembers he said his heart is made of stone, and she says, "I love you" and stabs him. Feyre chooses to kill the fairies, so she is giving up her soul.

Legendborn by Tracy Deonn

The old mother asks Bree why she wants to know her history. Bree answers that her mother's life counted, and she wants her death to count too. This is the same scene as the protagonist understands the story goal.

Bree sees Vera, the first of Bree's line, and asks for the strength to fight. She exchanges this strength for the lives of all future daughters, one daughter at a time. Bree is one of the future daughters. Bree has given up being an individual. She is connected to her ancestors and Vera's oath.

A Game of Thrones by George R. R. Martin

Arya, Eddard's daughter and part of the combined protagonist, has run away and is searching for food. She learns King Robert is dead. She's lost all of her belongings except what she's wearing and her sword, Needle. She hears the summoning bells. This leads her to the courtyard where her father is about to be executed. Arya is giving up life with her family.

Lead-Up to External Climax Patterns

The protagonists all give up something.

> Violet knows she is about to die, so she is giving up her life.
>
> Bella knows she must stay with Edward, so she gives up a life with her mother.
>
> Touraine chooses to reject Princess Luca's offer, so she is giving up her life.
>
> Feyre chooses to kill the fairies, so she is giving up her soul.
>
> Bree exchanges strength for the lives of all future daughters, so has given up her individuality.
>
> Arya has gone into hiding, so she's given up on being with her family.

Your Fun Task

Actions

For Outlining:

Create the main event for the reaction to the lead-up to the external climax and add it to your fantasy vault.

For Editing:

In one to two sentences, summarize the main event for the lead-up to the external climax and add it to your fantasy vault.

Decision

While outlining, make the following decision and add it to your fantasy vault:

- What is the protagonist willing to sacrifice?

Checklist

- Show what the protagonist is willing to sacrifice in order to achieve the goal in the climax.

Chapter Forty-One: External Climax

Show the protagonist either achieving or not achieving the story goal in the external skeleton blurb. This must be shown clearly to the reader, so the reader leaves the story satisfied.

Climax Scene Duties

The climax scene should:

1. Be told from the protagonist's point of view.

2. Be written in active form.

3. Show the protagonist leading the action.

4. Show the protagonist addressing the external story goal.

5. Mirror the inciting incident.

Fantasy Genre-Specific Duties

In a fantasy, the external and supernatural plots propel each other forward, and can be woven together in the climax.

Example Novels: External Climax

Fourth Wing by Rebecca Yarros

The wyvern arrive in force to support the venin, and the battle begins to save this city of Resson.

A venin lands on Tairn's back, and Violet kills the venin to protect Tairn. Violet and Xaden use their supernatural powers to defeat the venin and win the battle.

Liam dies.

External Skeleton Blurb: Violet must use her intelligence to fight other students in the Riders Quadrant; otherwise, she won't survive her first year as a cadet.

Violet achieved the external story goal and avoided the stakes: death.

Twilight by Stephenie Meyer

Bella tells her mother she wants to go back to Forks. This closes off the external goal of Bella learning to live in a new town with her father.

External skeleton blurb: Bella must learn to live with her father in a new town; otherwise, her mother will not have a new life.

Bella achieved the external story goal.

The Unbroken by C. L. Clark

Touraine kills Captain Rogan. He was part of the soldiers who came to stop the rebellion the Sands were building. She kills him using Brigāni magic because sacrifices must be made. She chooses her people over her army.

External Skeleton Blurb: Touraine must choose the winning side in the battle between the empire, her homeland, and the Shālan; otherwise, she will die.

Touraine achieved her external goal of choosing the winning side.

A Court of Thorns and Roses by Sarah J. Maas

Feyre solves the riddle: The answer is love. The curse is broken, and she knows she will never leave Prythian.

External Skeleton Blurb: Feyre must find a way to leave Prythian; otherwise, she will never see her family again.

Feyre failed to achieve the external goal because she doesn't return to her home with humans.

Legendborn by Tracy Deonn

The root magic and Arthur's magic come together. Vera (the oldest mother) arrives from the past because Bree calls her. Bree learns her history and that her mother died by accident.

External Skeleton Blurb: Bree must search for the truth about her mother's death; otherwise, she won't understand her heritage and how to live among the supernatural.

Bree achieved her external story goal.

A Game of Thrones by George R. R. Martin

Eddard Stark is executed by King Joffrey. Arya becomes a fugitive, and the War of the Five Kingdoms begins.

External Skeleton Blurb: The humans must choose who will sit on the throne; otherwise; the kingdoms will fall apart.

Eddard failed at keeping Robert on the throne. Joffrey succeeded in gaining the throne.

External Climax Patterns

In all six novels, the reader knows if the protagonist succeeded or failed at achieving their external story goal.

Your Fun Task

Actions

For Outlining:

Create the main event for the external climax and add it to your fantasy vault.

For Editing:

In one to two sentences, summarize the main event for the external climax and add it to your fantasy vault.

Decision

While outlining, make the following decision and add it to your fantasy vault:

- Will the protagonist achieve the external story goal?

Checklist

○ Show the protagonist addressing the external story goal.

Chapter Forty-Two: Reaction to the External Climax

This scene shows the reader how the climax affects the protagonist and other characters and often shows the protagonist wanting something they can't have.

Example Novels: Reaction to the External Climax

Fourth Wing by Rebecca Yarros

At the end of the climax scene, Andarna catches Violet. Violet has been poisoned. She is cut off telepathically from Xaden, Tairn, and Andarna, and it's torture for her. She thinks it might be better to die except that Xaden might die too. Xaden asks her to fight.

Note how the author makes the reaction scenes short relative to the other scenes, so the pace is fast. This is a powerful technique after the fast-paced climax sequence.

Twilight by Stephenie Meyer

In the external climax, Bella told her mother Edward was part of the reason she is staying in Forks. Edward overheard this. Bella's reaction to staying is that she makes Edward promise to never leave her. She asks him to turn her into a vampire and he refuses.

The Unbroken by C. L. Clark

Touraine wakes up in a tent (this is several scenes after the climax). She's been asleep for a month. She is with the priestess's wife. The priestess is dead, and her wife is dying. Touraine wants to stop the priestess's wife from dying but the healing magic won't work if the woman wants to die.

A Court of Thorns and Roses by Sarah J. Maas

Amarantha attacks Feyre. Feyre decides to die instead of saying she doesn't love Tamlin. Amarantha tortures her. Rhysand tries to help her but he isn't strong enough. Feyre found a new ally.

Legendborn by Tracy Deonn

After all the knowledge she's gained, Bree still wants to fight, and she is granted one final truth by the old mother. This leads her to the supernatural climax.

A Game of Thrones by George R. R. Martin

Eddard is killed in the climax, so he can't react. Yoren takes Arya with him. He keeps calling her boy. Arya needs to learn to be seen as a boy if she is to survive. He gives Arya's sword, Needle, back to her.

Reaction to the External Climax Patterns

In all six books, the protagonist wants something they can't have.

    Violet wants to die.

    Bella wants to turn into a vampire.

Touraine wants the priestess's wife to live.

Feyre wants Tamlin to attack Amarantha.

Bree wants to be accepted by others.

Arya wants to be with her family.

Your Fun Task

Actions

For Outlining:

Create the main event for the reaction to the external climax and add it to your fantasy vault.

For Editing:

In one to two sentences, summarize the main event for the reaction to the external climax and add it to your fantasy vault.

Decision

While outlining, make the following decision and add it to your fantasy vault:

- Will the protagonist want something they can't have?

Checklist

○ Show what the protagonist wants but can't have.

Chapter Forty-Three: Lead-Up to the Supernatural Climax

The protagonist learns something they need in the supernatural climax or they understand something about themselves.

This scene often shows the protagonist is willing to die.

Example Novels: Lead-Up to the Supernatural Climax

Fourth Wing by Rebecca Yarros

Violet learns that venin can channel power into wyvern. She needs this information to win the battle in the climax. Violet decides not to run from the battle and knows she might die.

Twilight by Stephenie Meyer

Bella understands she must die to protect those she loves. Her goal is not to live among vampires, it's dying for them so they can live. She plans to isolate herself with the evil vampire, so he stays away from the Cullens.

The Unbroken by C. L. Clark

Touraine tries to pray. She decides to die because she chooses to, and that death will come on her terms. This is the same scene as the lead-up to the external climax.

A Court of Thorns and Roses by Sarah J. Maas

Feyre feels a magical bond with Rhysand go tight. She sees herself through his eyes as she is dying.

Legendborn by Tracy Deonn

Bree learns her true history that she is Arthur's Scion, and Nick is not. She faces those who wish her dead with courage.

A Game of Thrones by George R. R. Martin

Daenerys plans to step onto Drogo's funeral pyre. She believes she is Dragonborn and the fire won't kill her. She steps bravely into the fire.

Lead-Up to the Supernatural Climax Patterns

All six books show the protagonist is willing to die for their cause.

> In *Fourth Wing*, Violet knows they will all die fighting but wants to save the people of Resson anyway.

> In *Twilight*, Bella draws the evil vampire away from the Cullens, so they can live.

> In *The Unbroken*, Touraine decides how she will die.

> In *A Court of Thorns and Roses*, Feyre sees herself die.

> In *Legendborn*, Bree faces her enemies with her sword drawn.

> In *A Game of Thrones*, Daenerys steps onto a funeral pyre.

Your Fun Task

Actions

For Outlining:

Create the main event for the lead-up to the supernatural climax and add it to your fantasy vault.

For Editing:

In one to two sentences, summarize the main event for the lead-up to the supernatural climax and add it to your fantasy vault.

Decision

While outlining, make the following decision and add it to your fantasy vault:

- Why is the protagonist willing to die for their cause?

Checklist

○ Show the protagonist facing death or willing to face death.

Chapter Forty-Four: The Supernatural Climax

The protagonist uses the supernatural to achieve the supernatural story goal.

Example Novels Supernatural Climax

Let's look at each of these scenes in the context of the supernatural skeleton blurbs.

Fourth Wing by Rebecca Yarros

Supernatural Plot: Violet must learn to control her signet; otherwise, she can't protect Navarre's borders from evil mythical creatures and all inside the borders will die.

Violet controls her lightning and kills the venin. This is the final major change in her use of the supernatural for book one in this series. She has achieved the supernatural story goal.

Violet learns that when she kills venin, the wyvern linked to that venin also dies. This is supernatural knowledge she needs in book two of the series.

The climax scene also contains the external climax scene.

Twilight by Stephenie Meyer

Supernatural Plot: Bella must learn to live among vampires; otherwise, she will not find her "Happy Ever After" life with Edward.

Bella faces the evil vampire, and he beats her bloody.

Bella addresses the supernatural goal that she must learn to live among vampires. The vampires save Bella, so she has successfully learned to live with them.

This scene occurs before the external climax. The readers will see this as the main climax of the story.

The Unbroken by C. L. Clark

Supernatural Plot: Touraine must learn Shālan magic; otherwise, her people will die.

Touraine gets the golden eyes and becomes a Brigāni. She kills Captain Rogan using magic.

This is the same scene as the external plot climax.

The supernatural story goal is achieved when Touraine uses the magic to defend herself.

A Court of Thorns and Roses by Sarah J. Maas

Supernatural Skeleton Blurb: Feyre must break an ancient curse; otherwise, she will doom her lover's world and she will die.

Feyre breaks the curse and has saved her lover's world.

Legendborn by Tracy Deonn

Supernatural Skeleton Blurb: Bree must combine Root magic with Legendborn magic; otherwise, the ancient ones will destroy the world.

Bree removes Excalibur from the stone. She understands she is Arthur's Scion and is a medium, therefore she has achieved her supernatural goal.

This is not the same scene as the external plot climax. This is the scene the readers will see as the main climax of the story.

A Game of Thrones by George R. R. Martin

Supernatural Skeleton Blurb: Daenerys must become the mother of dragons; otherwise, she won't become the Dothraki leader, and she will die.

The dragons are born, and Daenerys becomes the mother of dragons, therefore achieving her supernatural goal.

Supernatural Climax Patterns

The supernatural goal is addressed in all climax scenes.

The supernatural is used in all climax scenes.

The supernatural climax can be a standalone scene or combined with the external story arc scene.

> *Fourth Wing, The Unbroken, A Game of Thorns and Roses*: Both the external and supernatural goals are addressed in the same scene.

> *Twilight, Legendborn,* and *A Game of Thrones*: The supernatural climax is a standalone scene.

Your Fun Task

Actions

For Outlining:

Create the main event for the supernatural climax and add it to your fantasy vault.

For Editing:

In one to two sentences, summarize the main event for the supernatural climax and add it to your fantasy vault.

Decision

While outlining, make the following decision and add it to your fantasy vault:

- Will the protagonist achieve the supernatural story goal?

Checklist

○ Show the protagonist addressing the supernatural story goal.

○ Show the protagonist using the supernatural to address the supernatural story goal.

Chapter Forty-Five: Reaction to the Supernatural Climax

This scene shows how the supernatural climax impacts the protagonist.

Fantasy readers want to see the effect the supernatural climax has on the protagonist.

It's common for the protagonist to be unconscious or dead (but can be revived) in this scene.

Example Novels: Reaction to the Supernatural Climax

Fourth Wing by Rebecca Yarros

Violet is poisoned and is unconscious and dying. Xaden is desperate to save her.

Twilight by Stephenie Meyer

Bella is unconscious and dying. Edward arrives and sucks vampire poison out of her without killing her.

The Unbroken by C. L. Clark

Touraine wakes up in a tent (this is several scenes after the climax). She's been unconscious for a month. She is with the Brigāni and has returned to her mother. Her first thought after waking is about others.

Legendborn by Tracy Deonn

Bree doesn't want people to kneel to her. Nick kneels at her feet. She's gone past being his equal. She collapses while putting Excalibur back into the stone. Sel carries her unconscious body to William, the healer.

A Court of Thorns and Roses by Sarah J. Maas

Feyre is dead and sees her body through Rhysand's eyes. Tamlin kills Amarantha. The fairies bring Feyre back to life.

A Game of Thrones by George R. R. Martin

Daenerys simulated death by entering the funeral pyre. She has survived the fire and the people see her dragons. The people declare loyalty to the Khaleesi by saying, "Blood of my blood." This is also the closing image.

Reaction to the Supernatural Climax Patterns

In all six books the protagonist is either unconscious or temporarily dead.

In *Fourth Wing*, poison causes Violet to pass out.

In *Twilight*, the evil vampire sucks Bella's blood until she passes out.

In *Legendborn*, Bree passes out after returning Excalibur to the stone.

In *The Unbroken*, Touraine has been unconscious for a month.

In *A Court of Thorns and Roses*, Feyre is temporarily dead.

In *A Game of Thrones*, this is done slightly differently. Daenerys goes into the fire and the reader loses her for a while. This is a symbolic death.

In all but *A Game of Thrones,* another character helps the protagonist survive.

Your Fun Task

Actions

For Outlining:

Create the main event for the reaction to the supernatural climax and add it to your fantasy vault.

For Editing:

In one to two sentences, summarize the main event for the reaction to the supernatural climax and add it to your fantasy vault.

Decisions

While outlining, make the following decisions and add them to your fantasy vault:

- Will the protagonist be unconscious or temporarily dead?

- Which character will help them survive?

Checklist

○ Show the protagonist in some form of unconsciousness or death.

Chapter Forty-Six: Resolution

This scene(s) should show how the protagonist's world changed because of the events in the story. The reader must see the protagonist interacting with their new ordinary world.

This scene(s) shows a change in a relationship that is important to the protagonist.

Example Novels: Resolution

Fourth Wing by Rebecca Yarros

Xaden sits beside Violet's bed for three days while she recovers. Violet tells him she still loves him but no longer trusts him. They are bonded for life, but the relationship has changed forever.

Violet is fighting against the school instead of for the school. This happens right before the closing image.

Twilight by Stephenie Meyer

Edward takes Bella to the prom. The hook to the next book happens when Jacob shows up with a warning from the werewolves. Edward shows her that he wants to be part of her human life.

The Unbroken by C. L. Clark

The Balladairan ships leave Qazāl, and the Brigāni and the Sands are united. Touraine is no longer part of the army.

A Court of Thorns and Roses by Sarah J. Maas

Feyre learns she is a High Fae. Feyre and Tamlin finally get to unite. She pushes the horror of killing two Fae from her mind for now.

Legendborn by Tracy Deonn

Bree now lives in a world where some support her and some don't. Her life and Nick's are in grave danger. She teams up with Sel to find Nick, putting his safety before hers.

A Game of Thrones by George R. R. Martin

Four resolution scenes occur after the external climax and before the supernatural climax.

Bran Stark dreams of his father. He sees dragon glass for the first time and learns Eddard is dead.

Sansa Stark no longer wants to marry Joffrey and wants to go back to Winterfell. Joffrey takes her to see her father's head on a spike.

Tyrion Lannister's father calls him his son but only because he thinks Jaime is dead.

Robb Stark is chosen as King of the North.

The final resolution scene is the same scene as the closing image. Daenerys becomes the leader of the Dothraki.

A *Game of Thrones* uses a combined protagonist giving room in the story to show the resolution for more than one character.

Resolution Patterns

In this scene, there is a change to an important relationship. It grows stronger, weaker, or changes.

> Violet loves but doesn't trust Xaden.
>
> Edward wants to be part of Bella's human life and doesn't want her to be a vampire.
>
> Touraine has united the Sands and the Brigāni.
>
> Feyre and Tamlin unite.
>
> Bree teams up with Sel instead of Nick.
>
> Daenerys is the Khaleesi and the mother of dragons (a new relationship).

Your Fun Task

Actions

For Outlining:

Create the main event for the resolution and add it to your fantasy vault.

For Editing:

In one to two sentences, summarize the main event for the resolution and add it to your fantasy vault.

Decision

While outlining, make the following decision and add it to your fantasy vault:

- Which character will the protagonist change their relationship with?

Checklist

○ Show a change in a relationship that is important to the protagonist.

Chapter Forty-Seven: Closing Image

The closing image is the last visual the reader has of your story.

This is the same image for both the external and supernatural plots.

If possible, have it mirror the opening image.

Example Novels: Closing Image

Fourth Wing by Rebecca Yarros

Violet's brother, Brennan, is alive. This is the hook to book two.

The closing image mirrors the opening image. In the opening image, Violet is running toward the school to begin fighting for her life. She thinks there is a good chance she'll die that day. In the closing image, Violet lives and she meets her brother. He welcomes her to the revolution and a new life stretches out before her.

Twilight by Stephenie Meyer

Edward and Bella are happy for now. Bella asks Edward to turn her into a vampire and he refuses.

In the opening image, Bella's life is at stake as she's thinking about how she is about to die. The closing image is a mirror to the opening image because she is with Edward, a vampire, and he won't kill her.

The Unbroken by C. L. Clark

The opening image shows Touraine, landing in her home country as a cadet.

In the opening a sandstorm is brewing. In the closing image it's raining. In the opening image, Touraine is wearing her military uniform. In the closing image she is barefoot. The mirror occurs because the opening image shows Touraine working with a team. In the closing image she must face the troubles to come by herself.

In the closing image, Princess Luca has left Touraine's home country and Touraine must stay to get a system in place.

Touraine is left with Luca's letter to read. This is the hook for the next book.

Legendborn by Tracy Deonn

Bree leaves her court for a walk with Sel, swearing to save Nick because she loves him. She takes off running because she needs one moment to herself before the next journey begins.

In the opening image, Bree is with her father, learning about her mother's death. She is weak and lost. Nothing feels real to her. In the closing image, she is full of strength.

A Court of Thorns and Roses by Sarah J. Maas

Feyre and Tamlin go back to his home. Alis is there with her boys. The closing image mirrors the opening image. Feyre is safe in a home of abundance. In the opening, she is starving and in danger.

The hook to the next book comes earlier in the story when she agrees to spend a week each month with Rhysand. The reader wants to know how she'll balance life between Rhysand and Tamlin.

A Game of Thrones by George R. R. Martin

The people all declare loyalty to the Khaleesi by saying, "Blood of my blood." This is also the reaction to the supernatural climax and the hook for book two.

The final image is Daenerys standing strong with her dragons. The opening image shows the Night Watch men in a forest unaware that the supernatural exists. The mirror exists because we are shown people who don't know the supernatural exists and we end with people knowing it exists.

Closing Image Patterns

Five of the books put the hook to the next book in the series in the closing image. Only *A Court of Thorns and Roses* places the hook earlier in the story.

The opening image and closing images for all six books mirror each other.

Your Fun Task

Actions

For Outlining:

Create the main event for the closing image and add it to your fantasy vault.

For Editing:

In one to two sentences, summarize the main event for the closing image and add it to your fantasy vault.

Decision

While outlining, make the following decision and add it to your fantasy vault:

- What feeling do you want to leave the reader with?

Checklist

○ Mirror the opening image.

○ Post a review for Kristina and Lucy.

PART THREE
From Genre-Specific Scenes to Outlined Novel

SECRETS TO WRITING A FANTASY

Chapter Forty-Eight: The Story Arc Supporting Scenes

In part two of this book, we showed you the purpose of every genre-specific scene. In addition to that knowledge, you'll need a way to see the scenes in clusters. This will help you create the main events for the scenes surrounding the story arc scenes. From there you can go on to create the rest of the scenes your novel will need.

A cluster is a group of scenes that act like a single system. When you think of the lead-up to a story arc scene, the story arc scene, and the reaction to the story arc scene as a cluster, you can structure them for maximum reader engagement.

It's easier to do this after you've woven both the external and supernatural story arc scenes because you know the order of the scenes.

Background Theory

You've already created the main events for ten story arc scenes. The external plot story arc scenes give you the foundation for the external plot. The supernatural story arc scenes created the foundation for the supernatural plot. You've woven these together and have a strong view of your story. You know what each of the genre-specific scenes should do.

Let's build another level of your novel's foundation and look at scenes that support character development.

The scenes in the ordinary world, meaning everything before the inciting incident, show who the protagonist is at the story's start.

The lead-up and reaction to the story arc scenes are where you show character development and change. The lead-up to a story arc scene shows the character's motivation before the main event in the story arc scene. The reaction scene shows how the protagonist feels, acts, or changes because of the main event in the story arc scene.

The events in an external story arc scene will affect the character differently than the events in a supernatural story arc scene.

Other scenes that show character growth are the "Resistance to the Story Goal" and "Protagonist Understands the Story Goal." These two scenes can even mirror each other.

Resistance to the Story Goal and Protagonist Understands the Story Goal scenes can mirror each other and highlight character growth.

The scenes following the climax show who the protagonist is after they have addressed the combined story goal.

Fourth Wing: Story Arc Supporting Scenes

We're going to use *Fourth Wing* as an example. Here is a reminder of the story arc scenes. The percentages are approximate.

Fourth Wing Story Arcs

Supernatural Story Arc		External Story Arc
Climax		
Violet wins battle 90%		90% Violet wins battle
Plot Point 2		
Violet kills Jack using lightning 70%		70% Violet kills Jack using lightning
Middle Plot Point		
		58% Violet poisons Jack
Violet stops time through dragon 44%		
Plot Point 1		
Violet names dragons at Threshing 35%		
		21% Violet beats opponent with poison
Inciting Incident		
Dragon breathes fire on Violet 10%		
		Violet ordered to Riders Quadrant before story starts

This is going to help us create the main events for the scenes that are the lead-up and reactions to the story arc scenes.

Let's look at *Fourth Wing* in clusters.

Supernatural inciting incident

- Lead-up to the supernatural inciting incident
- Supernatural inciting incident: Dragon breathes fire on Violet.
- Reaction to the supernatural inciting incident

External Plot Point 1

- Lead-up to external plot point 1
- External plot point 1: Violet beats an opponent with poison
- Reaction to the external plot point 1

Supernatural Plot Point 1

- Lead-up to supernatural plot point 1
- Supernatural plot point 1: Violet names dragons at Threshing
- Reaction to supernatural plot point 1

Supernatural Middle Plot Point

- Lead-up to supernatural middle plot point
- Supernatural middle plot point: Violet stops time through her dragon
- Reaction to supernatural middle plot point

External Middle Plot Point

- Lead-up to external middle plot point
- External middle plot point: Violet poisons Jack
- Reaction to external middle plot point

Supernatural & External Plot Point 2

- Lead-up to supernatural & external plot point 2
- Supernatural & external plot point 2: Violet kills Jack using lightning
- Reaction to supernatural & external plot point 2

Supernatural & External Climax

- Lead-up to supernatural & external climax
- Supernatural & external climax: Violet wins battle
- Reaction to supernatural & external climax

This shows us the next level of structure in the story.

You don't have to create your story in this order. We find it helpful to break down an existing story so we can see why each of the scene purposes are important to a fantasy novel.

First, we'll create the main events for the scenes before and after the inciting incidents. Here are the duties of the inciting incidents. We covered each of these in-depth in part two of this book.

Duties

Supernatural Story Arc	External Story Arc

Reaction to the Inciting Incident

Shows a misbelief related to the supernatural story goal.

Reveals personality traits that will help or hinder the protagonist with the external story goal.

Inciting Incident

The protagonist believes in or uses the supernatural.

A challenge, a problem, or an adventure to undertake.

Lead-Up to the Inciting Incident

Show the protagonist's lack of power by putting them in a vulnerable situation.

Shows the protagonist's motivation to accept the external story goal.

Fourth Wing Supernatural Inciting Incident Clusters

We started with the supernatural inciting incident because the external inciting incident happens before page one. In *Fourth Wing*, there is no cluster for the external inciting incident. If your story shows the external inciting incident in action, you'll have a cluster for that too.

- Lead-up to the supernatural inciting incident: Xaden transfers Violet to his wing, Fourth Wing. This shows Xaden has the power and not Violet. She is at his mercy.

- Supernatural inciting incident: Dragon breathes fire on Violet.

- Reaction to the supernatural inciting incident: As the names of the dead are read, Violet realizes that everyone around her knows they could die at any time. This shows Violet still believes she won't survive the first year as a cadet.

Duties

Supernatural Story Arc	External Story Arc

Reaction to Plot Point 1

The protagonist shows they are stronger because of the event in plot point 1

Reveals personality traits that will help or hinder the protagonist with the external story goal

↑

Plot Point 1

The protagonist believes in or uses the supernatural

The protagonist accepts the adventure

↑

Lead-Up to Plot Point 1

The protagonist tries to be alone

A real or metaphorical death is a possible consequence of the main event

***Fourth Wing* Plot Point 1 Clusters**

We are revealing the clusters in the order they appear in *Fourth Wing*.

External Plot Point 1

- Lead-up to external plot point 1: Violet goes into the forest at night and collects plants she can turn into poison. This shows a real death could be coming.

- External plot point 1: Violet beats opponent with poison.

- Reaction to the external plot point 1: Xaden shows Violet how to win without poisoning her opponents. He demonstrates how to give a lethal blow using a dagger. This shows she needs help from others. Without learning to accept help, she won't achieve her external story goal.

Supernatural Plot Point 1

- Lead-up to supernatural plot point 1: Violet sees Jack and others tracking a small dragon. She warns the dragon. This opens the possibility that Violet lives or dies in the next scene.

- Supernatural plot point 1: Violet names dragons at Threshing.

- Reaction to supernatural plot point 1: Violet refuses to have her wound treated by the healer because she understands she can't appear weak. She is stronger because she bonded with two dragons.

Duties

Supernatural Story Arc   **External Story Arc**

Reaction to Middle Plot Point

Shows who the protagonist will trust

Show what the protagonist is afraid of

⬆

Middle Plot Point

Forces a risky decision

False victory or defeat

⬆

Lead-Up to Middle Plot Point

Shows the protagonist that they are missing trust from their lives

Last moment of safety before the protagonist faces death or puts someone they love in danger

Fourth Wing Middle Plot Point Clusters

Supernatural Middle Plot Point

- Lead-up to the supernatural middle plot point: Violet stands up to Jack, Dain, and Xaden, showing Tairn and

Andarna she's ready to channel their dragon powers. This shows Violet's strength and makes the next scene believable.

- Supernatural middle plot point: Violet stops time through a dragon.

- Reaction to supernatural middle plot point: Violet trusts Xaden with Andarna's secret.

External Middle Plot Point

- Lead-up to external middle plot point: Violet puts her own life in danger. She convinces Liam to keep Xaden busy while she fights Jack.

- External middle plot point: Violet poisons Jack.

- Reaction to external middle plot point: Violet is afraid her powers won't appear.

Duties

Supernatural Story Arc	External Story Arc
Reaction to Plot Point 2	
Shows the protagonist being worse off	Shows the protagonist choosing between two groups

⬆

Plot Point 2	
Shows the protagonist learning the supernatural limitations	Shows the protagonist facing dark forces

⬆

Lead-Up to Plot Point 2	
The protagonist tests trusting someone to help with the supernatural	Shows the protagonist or another character prepare to protect someone

Supernatural & External Plot Point 2 Cluster

- Lead-up to supernatural & external plot point 2: Xaden has a saddle made for Violet because she can't stay on her dragon.

- Supernatural & external plot point 2: Violet kills Jack using lightning.

- Reaction to supernatural & external plot point 2: Violet killed Jack and has to live with that. She is better off because she has her signet, but worse off because she understands her signet is meant to kill.

SECRETS TO WRITING A FANTASY

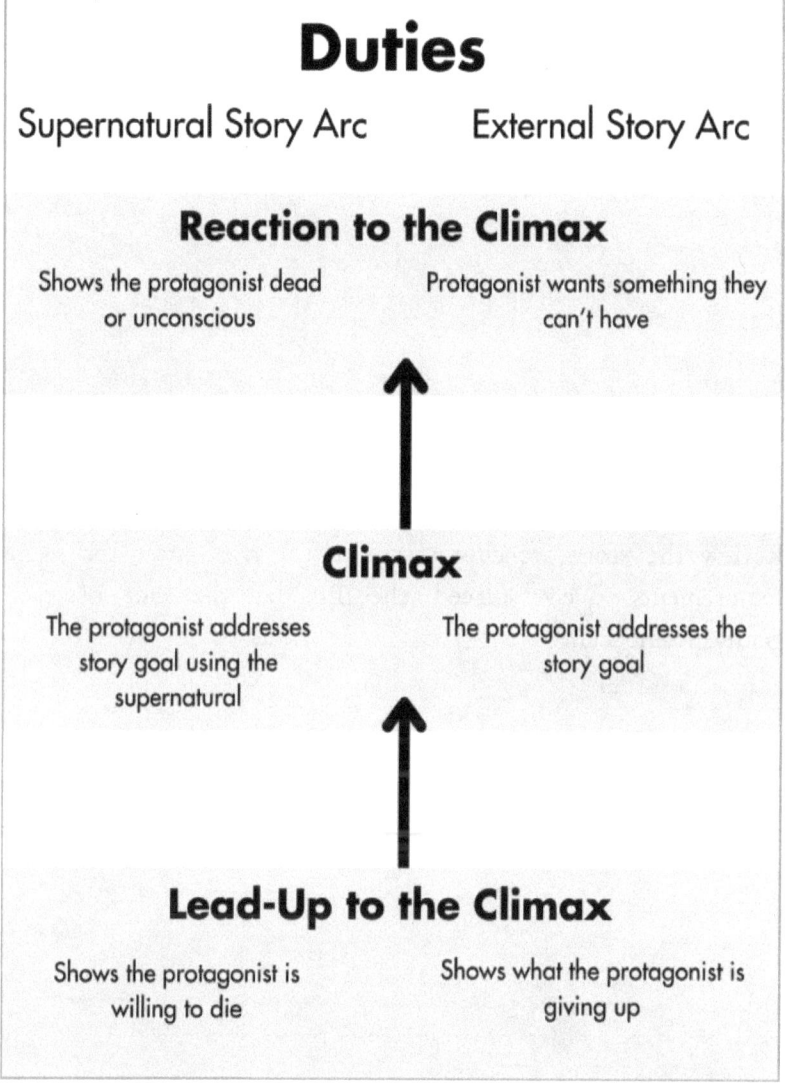

Supernatural & External Climax Cluster

- Lead-up to supernatural & external climax: Violet learns that venin can channel power into wyvern. She decides not to run from the battle and knows she might die.

- Supernatural & external climax: Violet wins the battle.

- Reaction to supernatural & external climax: Violet is poisoned, unconscious, and dying. She wants to die, and Xaden won't let her.

Your Fun Task

Actions

Review the story arc clusters and check they meet the scene requirements. We've placed checklists at the end of each genre-specific scene.

Chapter Forty-Nine: Are You Writing a Series or a Single Novel?

This is not a book about writing a series. Since stories in the fantasy genre are often told over a series of novels, we've included the ten decisions to make before you write your series. If you're writing a standalone book, you can skip this section. Or read on. Many writers, once they see how to structure a series, find they want to write another book in the world they created.

The first step in building your fantasy series is deciding between a closed or an open format.

Closed Series: This is a self-contained story told across a predetermined number of novels. Each book connects to the overall plot, leading to a satisfying conclusion in the last installment.

Open Series: The number of novels is open-ended, with stories linked by characters or the setting.

Decisions for Each Series Type:

The next steps depend on whether you're writing a closed or an open series.

Closed Series

Number of Novels: Decide on the number of books for your series story arc.

Skeleton Blurbs: Craft a series-wide skeleton blurb summarizing the overarching plot, and individual blurbs for each novel to showcase specific plot points. For a fantasy series, in addition to individual skeleton blurbs, crafting a series skeleton blurb will solidify your overarching story arc and keep you on track for an epic series climax.

Story Arc Scenes: Outline the major plot points (story arc scenes) for both the entire series and each novel.

Open Series

Uniting Factor: Determine what will connect your novels: a central character, a specific world, or a combination of both.

Skeleton Blurbs: Write skeleton blurbs for the first three books. Consider creating a template (generic series skeleton blurb) that you can adapt for each book.

Story Arc Scenes: Outline the main events within the story arc scenes for the first three novels.

Testing Your Series Idea

Once you've chosen the type of series you're writing, written the skeleton blurbs, and outlined the story arc scenes, you have decisions to make at the scene level.

The **first scene-level decision** is what the opening and closing images will show in the setup and resolution of each novel.

The **second scene-level decision** is what type of protagonist you're going to use.

You've got three choices. The protagonist can be a single, combined, or group protagonist for each novel. In a series, you can write the novels using the same or different protagonist types. We call this the protagonist strategy.

The **third scene-level decision** is what POV strategy you're going to follow.

You'll choose whether you're writing from a single POV or from multiple POVs.

The **fourth scene-level decision** is whether to write the narrative in the first, second, or third person. We call this the narrative strategy.

The **fifth scene-level decision** is what tense you're going to write each scene in. You'll write in the past or present tense. You may even write in a combination of past and present tense. That's your artistic choice.

Our book *Secrets to Writing a Series* covers this in detail.

Everything you learned in this book can be used for each book in your series.

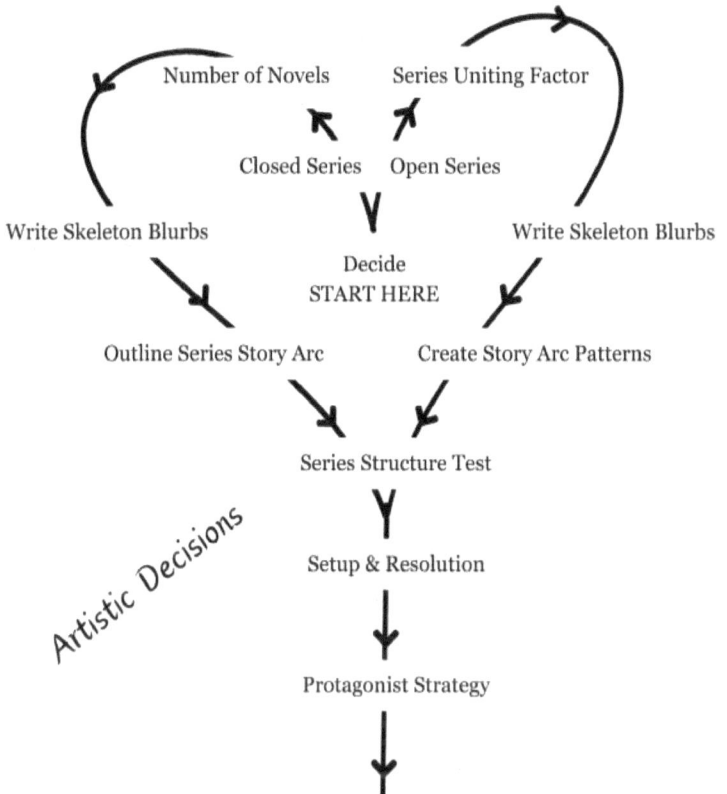

Appendix: Fantasy Decisions

For every scene, you'll make the following decisions:

- Where will this event be located relative to other scenes?
- How much page time does the event need?

The following shows the decisions that are specific to each scene.

Opening Image

- Will the supernatural be included in the opening image?
- Does the protagonist know about the supernatural?
- Will the opening image be a prologue, flashforward, or chapter?
- Will the opening image be a scene on its own or within another scene?

Lead-Up to the External Inciting Incident

- Will this scene come before, after, or be part of the supernatural inciting incident?

External Inciting Incident

- Will the supernatural be included in the external inciting incident?
- Does the protagonist physically leave their ordinary world?

- Will the external exciting incident happen before the story starts or after?

Reaction to the External Inciting Incident

- Will the supernatural be included in this scene?

Lead-Up to the Supernatural Inciting Incident

- Will this scene occur before, after, or in the external inciting incident scene?

Supernatural Inciting Incident

- Where will this scene be in your story relative to the external inciting incident?

Reaction to the Supernatural Inciting Incident

- Will the protagonist's reaction to the supernatural inciting incident be positive or negative?

Resistance to the Story Goal

- Will the resistance to both the external and the supernatural story goals be in the same scene or separate scenes?

Lead-Up to the External Plot Point 1

- Will the scene show a real or metaphorical death is the possible consequence?

External Plot Point 1

- Does this scene come before or after the supernatural plot point 1?

Reaction to the External Plot Point 1

- What character trait will help or hinder the protagonist in achieving their external story goal?

Lead-Up to the Supernatural Plot Point 1

- How will this time alone put the protagonist in peril?

Supernatural Plot Point 1

- What supernaturally significant event occurs for the protagonist?

Reaction to the Supernatural Plot Point 1

- How will the protagonist be stronger?

Goal Attempts

- Will this scene strengthen or weaken the protagonist?

- Will the protagonist attempt to achieve the external goal, the supernatural goal, or both?

- Will the goal attempts be a sentence, paragraph, scene or chapter in length?

Lead-Up to the External Middle Plot Point

- Will the protagonist put their own life in danger or someone else's?

External Middle Plot Point

- Will the scene contain supernatural elements?

Reaction to the External Middle Plot Point

- How will you show the protagonist being proactive instead of reactive?

Lead-Up to the Supernatural Middle Plot Point

- Will the protagonist lack trust in themselves or in another character?

Supernatural Middle Plot Point

- Does this scene come before, after, or in the same scene as the external middle plot point?

Reaction to the Supernatural Middle Plot Point

- Which character will the protagonist trust?

External Pressures

- How will each external pressure make it hard for the protagonist to achieve the story goal?

Lead-Up to the External Plot Point 2

- Who is the protagonist trying to protect?

External Plot Point 2

- What does the protagonist learn?

- What dark forces do they face?

Reaction to the External Plot Point 2

- Will the protagonist choose between two groups or will they connect two groups?

Lead-Up to the Supernatural Plot Point 2

- What does the protagonist learn about another character?

Supernatural Plot Point 2

- What knowledge does the protagonist gain about the supernatural?

Reaction to the Supernatural Plot Point 2

- Will the protagonist be worse off because they have harmed themselves or someone else?

Protagonist Understands the Story Goal

- Which story goal will the protagonist alter?

Lead-Up to the External Climax

- What is the protagonist willing to sacrifice?

External Climax

- Will the protagonist achieve the external story goal?

Reaction to the External Climax

- Will the protagonist want something they can't have?

Lead-Up to the Supernatural Climax

- Why is the protagonist willing to die for their cause?

Supernatural Climax

- Will the protagonist achieve the supernatural story goal?

Reaction to the Supernatural Climax

- Will the protagonist be unconscious or temporarily dead?
- Which character will help them survive?

Resolution

- Which character will the protagonist change their relationship with?

Closing Image

- What feeling do you want to leave the reader with?

Appendix: Fantasy Checklist

Opening image

- Introduce the protagonist.

- Show the ordinary world.

- Show what's at stake for the protagonist or what they are leaving behind in their ordinary world.

- Introduce the journey the protagonist is going on (this can also be in Chapter 1).

Lead-Up to External Inciting Incident

- Show the main event is related to the external story goal.

- Show the protagonist's motivation to accept the external story goal.

External Inciting Incident

- Contains new information about the story goal.

- Changes the story direction.

- Raises the stakes.

- Is full of tension (even in the quieter scenes).

- Is written in the protagonist's POV.

- Causes the protagonist to react to the action. The reaction is the start of the protagonist's journey.

- Is early in the story.

- Is related to the story goal stated in the external plot skeleton blurb.

- Presents the protagonist with a challenge, a problem, or an adventure to undertake.

Reaction to the External Inciting Incident

- Show the protagonist's reaction to the main event in the external inciting incident. Specifically, to the challenge, problem, or adventure.

- Reveal personality traits that will help or hinder the protagonist when they try to achieve the external story goal.

Lead-Up to the Supernatural Inciting Incident

- Show the protagonist's lack of power by putting them in a vulnerable situation.

- Show why the protagonist needs the supernatural to achieve their external story goal.

Supernatural Inciting Incident

- Occurs before both the external and supernatural plot point 1 scenes.

- Show the protagonist interacting with the supernatural.

- Is full of tension (even in the quieter scenes).

- Cause the protagonist to react to the action.

- Is related to the story goal stated in the supernatural skeleton blurb.

Reaction to the Supernatural Inciting Incident

- Show an external reaction to the supernatural inciting incident.

- Show an internal reaction to the supernatural inciting incident.

- Show a misbelief about their abilities that relate to the supernatural story goal.

Resistance to the Story Goal

- Show an external reaction to the supernatural inciting incident.

- Show an internal reaction to the supernatural inciting incident.

- Show a misbelief about their abilities that relate to the supernatural story goal.

Lead-Up to the External Plot Point 1

- Show what motivated the protagonist not to walk away from the external story goal.

- Hint a real or metaphorical death coming in plot point 1.

External Plot Point 1

- Show the protagonist accepting the adventure.
- Contain new information about the story goal.
- Change the story direction.
- Raise the stakes.
- Is full of tension.
- Is written in the protagonist's POV.

Reaction to the External Plot Point 1

- Show how the protagonist feels as a result of the main event in the external plot point 1 scene.
- Show a character trait that is different from the character trait shown in the reaction to the external inciting incident.

Lead-Up to the Supernatural Plot Point 1

- Foreshadow the protagonist's life could be at stake in the supernatural plot point 1.
- Make the supernatural plot point 1 be believable.
- Show the protagonist alone or their desire to be alone.

Supernatural Plot Point 1

- The supernatural is part of this scene.

- Show the protagonist accepting the supernatural goal.
- Foreshadow an event in the supernatural climax.

Reaction to the Supernatural Plot Point 1

- Show the protagonist getting stronger.
- Make the story stakes clear.

Goal Attempts

- Place scene after the plot point 1 for the respective plot goal attempts.
- Show the main event for the three goal attempts in any order:
- Show the protagonist learning to trust someone–positively or negatively.
- Show the protagonist learning from history–understanding the lesson or not.
- Show the protagonist learning from their actions–being successful or not.

Lead-Up to the External Middle Plot Point

- Show the protagonist's life or someone else's life is in danger.

External Middle Plot Point

- Be told from the protagonist's point of view.

- Be written in active form.

- Show the protagonist leading the action by the end of the scene.

- Show the protagonist proactively wanting to address the story goal.

- Foreshadow the ending.

- Show the protagonist facing a hard moment.

- Show a false victory or defeat.

Reaction to the External Middle Plot Point

- Show what the protagonist is afraid of.

Lead-Up to the Supernatural Middle Plot Point

- Show an event that makes the upcoming supernatural middle plot point believable.

- The protagonist is in this scene.

- The scene occurs before the supernatural middle plot point.

- Show the protagonist is missing trust from their life.

Supernatural Middle Plot Point

- Show the protagonist learning something about the supernatural.

- Show the protagonist engaging with or driving the supernatural storyline forward.

- Show the protagonist making a risky decision that is related to the supernatural and changes the story's direction.

Reaction to the Supernatural Middle Plot Point

- Show the protagonist trusting another character.

- Show the protagonist engaging with or driving the supernatural storyline forward.

- Show the protagonist making a risky decision that is related to the supernatural and changes the story's direction.

External Pressures

- Show the protagonist being distracted from their external or supernatural story goal.

Lead-Up to the External Plot Point 2

- Show the protagonist making preparations to protect someone.

External Plot Point 2

- Show the protagonist learning something that will help or hinder them in the climax scene.

Reaction to the External Plot Point 2

- Show the protagonist choosing between two groups or connecting two groups.

Lead-Up to the Supernatural Plot Point 2

- Show the protagonist trusting another character regarding something that is critical in the climax scene.

Supernatural Plot Point 2

- Show the protagonist gaining knowledge about the supernatural that they can use in the climax or show them facing the first major limitation of the supernatural.

Reaction to the Supernatural Plot Point 2

- Show the protagonist in a worse state than before the supernatural plot point 2.

Protagonist Understanding the Story Goal

- Show the protagonist altering one of their story goals.

Lead-Up to the External Climax

- Show what the protagonist is willing to give to win in the climax.

External Climax

- Show the protagonist addressing the external story goal.

Reaction to the External Climax

- Show what the protagonist wants but they can't have.

Lead-Up to the Supernatural Climax

- Show the protagonist facing death or willing to face death.

Supernatural Climax

- Show the protagonist addressing the supernatural story goal.

- Show the protagonist using the supernatural to address the supernatural story goal.

Reaction to the Supernatural Climax

- Show the protagonist in some form of unconsciousness.

Resolution

- Show a change in a relationship that is important to the protagonist.

Closing Image

- Mirror the opening image.

- Post a review for Kristina and Lucy.

Acknowledgments

K. Stanley

Thank you to L. Cooke for co-authoring our fourth book together.

Thank you to our copyeditor, Linda O'Donnell.

Mostly, thank you to Mathew, my husband and lifelong partner in everything. Without him, none of this has meaning.

L. Cooke

Thank you to K. Stanley, you have been an inspiration from start to finish. Thank you.

Linda O'Donnell. You make our writing stronger. Thank you.

Thank you to all of you who want to write fantasy stories. Please write them.

Thank you to my parents. Your generosity knows no bounds.

My boys, I love that you love fighting dragons, meeting bagpipe-playing gnomes, and going on mega adventures at your Friday meetups with your D&D friends. Thank you for giving me the time to write this book.

And to my husband, Andrew, I love you. And can we plant an arboreal Ogham-henge in the lower field–wouldn't that be magic? Thank you for taking control of the chores whilst I write.

About the Authors

K. Stanley

Combining her degree in computer mathematics with her success as a best-selling, award-winning author and fiction editor, K. Stanley founded Fictionary and is the CEO. Fictionary helps writers and editors create better stories faster with software, an online community, and training.

Her novels include The Stone Mountain Mystery Series. Her first novel, *Descent*, was nominated for the 2014 Arthur Ellis Unhanged Arthur for excellence in crime writing. *Descent* is also published in Germany by Luzifer-Verlag.

Blaze was shortlisted for the 2014 Crime Writers' Association Debut Dagger.

Her short stories are published in *The Ellery Queen Mystery Magazine*, and *Voices from the Valleys*. Her short story *When a Friendship Fails* won the Capital Crime Writer award.

Secrets to Editing Success, Secrets to Outlining a Novel, Secrets to Writing a Series, Secrets to Writing a Fantasy, The Author's Guide to Selling Books to Non-Bookstores, and *Your Editing Journey* are her non-fiction books.

L. Cooke

L. Cooke is a Fictionary Certified StoryCoach Editor. Lucy is the co-author of *Secrets to Editing Success, Secrets to Outlining A Novel, Secrets to Writing a Series,* and *Secrets to Writing a Fantasy.*

She is writing her first novel, *My Fairy Assassin.*

www.ingramcontent.com/pod-product-compliance
Lightning Source LLC
Chambersburg PA
CBHW030518230426
43665CB00010B/661